Greater Hamilton

MUSICIAN

Great City. Great Music. Great Musicians

I0163468

LORI YATES
By Kathryn Dunmore

DANIELLE BEAUDIN
By David Simpson
HARVEST PICNIC
By Tom Shea
HAMILTON'S
MUSIC LEGACY
By Jeffrey Martin
MOHAWK COLLEGE
MUSIC PROGRAM
By James Tennant

FUND YOUR OWN
MUSIC VIDEO

ALEX MACDOUGALL
MEMORIAL

ISSUE 2 VOL 1 2014

CAN $4.44

6 27843 35012 5

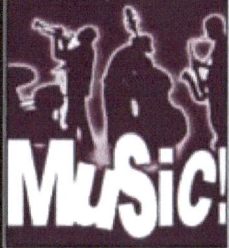

Greater Hamilton
MUSICIAN
ISSUE 2 VOL 1 2014

COVER STORY

8 LORI YATES
THE COUNTRY SINGER TALKS ABOUT HER CAREER TO DATE

FEATURES

10 MOHAWK COLLEGE
MOHAWK'S THREE-YEAR APPLIED MUSIC DIPLOMA PROGRAM EVOLVES WITH THE MUSIC INDUSTRY

14 DANIELLE BEAUDIN
THE SINGER TALKS ABOUT HER DEBUT ALBUM WAIT FOR YOUR LOVE

16 HAMILTON'S MUSIC LEGACY
A LOOK BACK THROUGH HAMILTON'S MUSICAL HERITAGE

24 HARVEST PICNIC
THIS YEAR'S FESTIVAL IN BRIEF

32 HAMILTON MUSIC AWARDS
THE 2013 AWARD WINNERS

40 ZIMFIRI POLOZ
ARTISTIC DIRECTOR OF THE HAMILTON CHILDREN'S CHOIR TALKS ABOUT THEIR RECENT TRIP TO GUANGZHOU CHINA

FRONTLINE

4 NEWS

7 A YEAR IN REVIEW

22 FREEDOM TRAIN

25 HARRISON KENNEDY FUNDRAISER

28 ALEX MACDOUGALL MEMOIR

30 ONLINE DIY

34 JUKASA STUDIOS

38 AN INSTRUMENT FOR EVERY CHILD

FILTER

13 GILLIAN NICOLA
HAMILTON MUSIC STRATEGY

20 FUNDING YOUR MUSIC VIDEO

21 HAMILTON'S RECORD STORES

26 UNDERGROUND & INDIE BANDS

31 FENIAN FILMS

33 THRESHOLD STUDIOS

35 BIG JOHNNY BLUE

42 DUNDAS VALLEY ORCHESTRA

44 CLASSIFIEDS

EDITOR-IN-CHIEF Glen T Brown
MANAGING EDITOR Jeffrey C. Martin
ART DIRECTOR & DESIGNER Cormac Figgis

PRINTER Premier Impressions INC

GBR Publications
115 Adeline Avenue, Hamilton, ON, L8H 5T5

Distributed through select magazine outlets and music industry locations in Hamilton, Burlington, Oakville, Brantford and Oshweken

ISSN 2292-1338 / ISBN 978-0-9936186-0-4

Comments, writing and advertising queries may be sent to glen@gbrpublications.com
More local musician news can be found at www.hamiltonmusician.com
© 2013 by GBR Publications

BRIGHT LIGHTS
EDITOR'S LETTER

It's time to celebrate the Greater Hamilton music scene. Any way you look at it – by genre, person, venue, song – it's pure gold; more than any tourist brochure or awards show can describe. Great musicians shine forth from our past and are bright lights in our present. In this second edition of Greater Hamilton Musician, we've highlighted Lori Yates. She shines in our singer-songwriter community. Many other brilliant people, ensembles, organizations and businesses are here too. What makes our scene special is that musicians in this town know each other and they support one another.

Mohawk College's Applied Music program is a beacon for young, new talent. The stream of musical entrepreneurs graduating reflects the vision of its stellar teaching team. Read more in this issue. Learn about recording facilities, our musical history, current events, and take in some technical tips. It's pretty rich. So much talent. So many new recordings. So many shows and festivals. It boggles the mind. I hope this publication will help you recognize, affirm, and support our wealth of musical talent. Enjoy reading!

Glen Brown publisher
GREATER HAMILTON MUSICIAN

JEFFREY C. MARTIN
Writer and PR-marketing pro, Jeff Martin is owner of Quorum Communications Inc. and senior communications counsel with Hamilton marketing agency Pier 8 Group. He's a member of the Professional Writers Association of Canada and is co-singer-songwriter of Hamilton roots act, The Caretakers.

CHRIS COWSILL
Hamilton guitarist-singer Christian Cowsill has performed professionally since 1994. He studied with some of Canada's top musicians and graduated from Mohawk College's Applied Music program in 2000. He's a freelance music teacher and Hamilton Arts Award winner.

TOM SHEA
Writer, poet, musician and teacher; Tom Shea teaches English, writers' craft, guitar, recording technology and drama at Saltfleet High School. He writes and records music, and is the creator of the local music blog *Hundred Mile Microphone*.

JAMES TENNANT
Jamie Tennant has written for The Hamilton Spectator, TV Times, SOCAN Words & Music, Toronto Sun, Chart Magazine and Hamilton Magazine. Program director at 93.3 CFMU FM, he also hosts music program "Ensemble!" and appears weekly on The Beat segment of Hamilton Life.

JOHN BEST
John Best is the founding publisher of the Bay Observer, a monthly news and opinion publication serving Hamilton and Burlington. As president of Best Communications Group, he provides strategic communications counsel to management in both the public and private sectors.

KATHRYN DUNMORE
Kathryn Dunmore has been writing about music for more than 10 years – the majority of her profiles featuring local artists from the Hamilton-Burlington area. She also works to promote causes important to her such as children and animal welfare.

LUKE CUMMINS
Freelance writer and blogger Luke Cummins has collected insightful and rare interviews with new and celebrated artists worldwide. His newest project is a collection of short stories, photography and music, with a connectivity and discussion focus.

BILL WATSON
Hamilton photographer Bill Watson captures "the" moment – his photos tell stories. A self-taught, '70s kind-of-photographer, he's old school and true to the cliché, "A picture's worth 1,000 words." Wedding, portrait, landscape, commercial or live concerts, Bill tells your story.

DAVID FAWCETT
An associate composer of the Canadian Music Centre, David Fawcett was a professional classical singer. He taught music in schools including 13 seasons as conductor and chorus master of Buchanan Park Opera Club.

IVAN SORENSEN
Hamilton's Ivan Sorensen specializes in portraiture, event, concert and band/performer photography. All about music-related photography, the challenge of capturing musicians in action is invigorating. If you see him shooting a concert or musical event, say hello.

BILJANA NJEGOVAN
Creator, writer, designer, editor and publisher of Hamilton music blog Cut From Steel, Biljana Njegovan brings a worldwide lens and local focus. Cut From Steel is one of the city's best sources for the newest music and music news.

KATHLEEN FARLEY
Computer geek, teacher, learner, greyhound rescuer, cat lover, vinyl junkie (1600+ records and counting), hockey fan, vegetarian, recovering non-profit executive, Kathleen Farley teaches technology skills at Toronto's Harris Institute and posts online tech training videos under the moniker Robobunnyattack.

KEVIN BARBER
Mohawk College Broadcast Journalism graduate, Kevin Barber worked as a journalist, marketer and video producer. Turning his passion for music into the notorious rock band Captain Easy, he then founded Hamilton's BOXO Studio. He serves singer-songwriter and session musicians with vibe-heavy recordings and high-quality video production.

PETER HILL
A McMaster University graduate, Peter Hill is also an inductee of the McMaster Alumni Gallery of Distinction. He served two terms as president of the Dundas Valley Orchestra and authored "The Dundas Valley Orchestra: A Jewel in the Valley."

SYMPHONY FOR THE DEVIL

Spending more time in L.A. this past year is paying off for director/producer Ryan Furlong (Fenian Films). His freshly penned unscripted one-hour music series, Symphony for the Devil, is getting some serious attention.

When asked about the essential content of "Symphony," Furlong said, "The show will break ground by breaking genre and creating something new, exciting and exclusive. Brilliant producers engaging celebrity musicians with the combined goal of cutting a fresh exclusive cover of a popular song (in a landmark studio). It all ends with a pop-up concert at unlikely public spots in large cities. Just imagine throwing Tom Waits into a studio with, backed by Daft Punk doing a cover of Madonna's "Like a Virgin."

Furlong has done a lot of video shooting in studios, and he's seen many unique characters and the way they engage and interact with musicians to get very specific results.

Great ideas create a buzz fast and, after his Hollywood stay found him meeting with a-list talent and studios, it only took one day back in Hamilton for the phone to ring with excited names seeking "attachment". He was reluctant to go into too much detail at this stage of development since "the winds may change" as he put it, but they include the likes of David Bowie's musical director, Gerry Leonard "among other brilliant and enthusiastic minds". It's the first successful step in "packaging" the series. This will be one reality show not to be missed.

LAURA COLE: THIS STAGE FEELS LIKE HOME

Laura Cole has soaked up the musical culture that has surrounded her all her life. Laura knows Daniel Lanois as Uncle Danny, through his friendship with her parents, and he's been listening to her sing since she was a kid. Her unmistakable talent for expressive, bluesy vocals and her natural comfort with being on stage has her performing regularly in local venues and festivals. Cole won the Galaxie Rising Star Award at the 2013 Burlington Sound of Music Festival.

Cole went to Los Angeles with Lanois to record a demo and get some extra experience and feedback. She muses, "I knew he would be someone who would be a little bit tougher on me."

Her first full album of original material, recorded at Porcelain Records, is due for release. Mark McLean (drums), Steve Bigas (guitar), Chris Chiarcos (bass) and Ron Cole (keyboards) backed her up. Describing the music she says, "The style is what we're calling 'voodoo rock,' like a mix between Motown and a Tom Waits vibe. Every song is coming across perfectly, with how the melody and lyrics fit together. It will reach a broad spectrum of people."

Cole and her dad recuperated together after being injured in a car crash by a drunk driver in 2009. Making music was like therapy. "Nothing makes me feel better than being on stage. My body and soul all connects for me when I'm singing, People ask me why I sing barefoot on stage. I tell them it feels like home."

TONGUE FU THE NEW DICTATORS

Tongue Fu recently recorded its debut album at Hamilton's Porcelain Records. The band considers itself a proud Hamilton rock 'n' roll six-pack who have a genuine fond admiration for hard rock 'n' roll.

Considering Tongue Fu is heavily influenced by American proto-punk rock band, the Dictators, it made logical sense to invite Andy Shernoff to be producer of this record. "I wanted no one other than Shernoff, who was their main songwriter, to be the producer of our debut," said Molinaro. "His production work includes not only the Dictators, but also Master Plan, Manitoba's Wild Kingdom, the Barracudas, Guided By Voices, Waldos and the Smithereens."

Tongue Fu formed in late 2012 and made their debut performance in January 2013. The band consists of Gord Lewis (Teenage Head), Gene Champagne (the Killjoys), Rob Sweeney (Durango 95/Purple Toads), Dave Elley (Orphans), Greg Brisco (Dinner Belles) and Lou Molinaro (co-owner and talent buyer of This Ain't Hollywood). Most show nights, you can find "the FU" hanging out at their James Street North digs… This Ain't Hollywood.

"Our mission is fuelled primarily by our selfish need and love for REAL rock 'n' roll," quips Molinaro. "It also provides us the therapeutic necessities for 'escaping reality.' We really do appreciate each other's company while we write and create music. So Tongue Fu is like an alternate galaxy that we enjoy visiting."

While swayed by liked-minded hardcore rock 'n' rollers such as Blue Oyster Cult, Radio Birdman, Alice Cooper, MC5, Teenage Head and the Dictators, Tongue Fu's recorded words and music demonstrate the band is indeed evolving its own sound and direction. And there's even a few heart wrenchers.

Look for the release of Tongue Fu's debut record in late winter 2014.

MUSIC LIVES ON AT THE HCA

The Hamilton Conservatory For The Arts (HCA), originally established as the Hamilton Conservatory of Music, has been a centre for musical and artistic excellence since its founding in 1905. Performers testify time and again about the superior acoustics in the upper performance hall. In keeping with its mission to be a community leader in artistic excellence, HCA is presenting several world-class piano concerts in 2014, including André LaPlante and Valerie Tryon.

More exciting is time-tested children's program now available at HCA. The Yamaha Music Education Program is a proven, developmentally appropriate method of music education for children as young as two. The "Tunes For Twos" program offers a mix of music, singing, movement and rhythm in a fun mix that encourages children to develop and internalize their love of music. Music Wonderland is for three- and four-year olds and Junior Music is for four- and five-year olds. "We're fortunate to have Teresa Sanecki as our Yamaha Music Faculty," said HCA Artistic Director Vitek Wincza. "Teresa has been teaching the Yamaha Music curriculum to children and adults for over 35 years."

ANDRÉ BISSON RHYTHM & BLUES EXPERIENCE

Touring with André Bisson & the J-Tones this past summer has been a perfect example of the life of an on-the-go musician from Hamilton. Loretta Hale is the band's tour manager and trumpet player. "Our very rewarding journey took us all the way to Wales and England," said Hale. "We feel so lucky and fulfilled to do what we love best for a living. It's great to have all the support from family, friends and our music-loving fans."

There's no question that the blues has re-emerged prominently in Hamilton. The city's has its share of Juno award-winning blues artists (Steve Strongman) and Maple Blues winners (Steve Strongman, Harrison Kennedy). In addition, the newly rejuvenated Hamilton Blues Society is becoming a supportive, connecting organizations for the local blues scene.

But André & the J-Tones have an interesting perspective on this topic. As the band toured, Hale noticed people making comments like, "What's in that Hamilton water?" and "How can I buy all the Canadian blues records?" "When we settled in Hamilton in 2002, we watched the Hamilton blues community start to grow and expand fantastically into 2013," said Hale. "We feel very lucky to have watched this."

The band is preparing for two tours in 2014. Frontman André Bisson's new album "Bad Scene," is out and Hale is busy sending out radio and review submissions. The J-Tones are getting ready to record again in 2014. "André Bisson was nominated for the 2013 Hamilton Music Awards for Blues Recording of the Year and for a few industry awards. We couldn't feel more lucky and proud."

RADIO FREE UNIVERSE

Currently ranked the number one music act in Canada and number five on the planet by ReverbNation, Radio Free Universe is shaping up to be one of the most influential new rock acts.

The band has gone viral after being nominated two years in a row for Hamilton Music Awards Best Rock Recording category. The new record, "13 Day Hangover," is a full-length follow up to their EP "Six" and fuses contemporary production with all the great classical elements a modern rock act needs to bring a distinctive voice to their sound.

Lead singer George Panagopoulos left LA in 2006 with the intent of finding all the elements to create a great rock band. It took some time and travelling, but after an unprecedented search, he found that Hamilton had what he needed: tons of venues with die-hard rock fans and above all, unbelievable talent – everywhere. Radio Free Universe was soon founded with veteran Hamilton guitar player Marcus Star. After two years of writing new songs, they've forged an incredible live show and recorded two albums with co-writers Ryan Davie (bass) and Ashton Norman (drums).

The show has been described as a freight train traveling at light speed. "It's all about the live performance," said Panagopoulos. "Something happens when we play, I can't explain it. What I love about Hamilton is that it's a tough city. If people like you here then you have a chance. It's made us work harder, it's made us rehearse more, and it's made us better."

HAMILTON MUSICIANS GUILD 110TH YEAR

The Hamilton Musicians Guild, Local 293 of the American Federation of Musicians (AFM), is celebrating its 110th year of serving Hamilton musicians. The Guild has seen steady growth in 2013, with a total 400 active members. This success story is attributed to the commitment of the Guild executive to rebuilding the aspects of the union that focus on serving members.

The Guild held an informative public seminar called Survival in Today's Music Business in February with special panelist Ian Thomas. The Spectator's Graham Rockingham hosted the event. Musicians were challenged to consider new opportunities for selling their music and how to maximize their efforts. For example, music is always being sought for the vast numbers of new independent movies and television programs in production. Local band Trickbag, shared how they successfully licensed their music.

The Guild acts on behalf of its members who book gigs in the US. The Federation works with governments of both countries to help cut through the "red tape" usually associated with obtaining work visas in either country. Member benefits include pension programs, local agreements for symphony work, contract templates, political advocacy as well as a subscription to the monthly International Musician magazine. Members also have access to a musical instrument and equipment insurance plan.

The Hamilton Musicians Guild has worked to better the position of local musicians. As a collective unit, members not only have a strong voice in collective bargaining and government lobbying, but anywhere musicians work.

HAMILTON BLUES SOCIETY TRIES OUT ITS NEW DIGS

Thanks to the Knights of Columbus, the Hamilton Blues Society (HBS) has a great home for their jams and other blues shows. It also includes meeting space for the society's executive.

The first of the revitalized monthly jams was on July 7, 2013. The jams have taken place on the third Sunday of each month since then, and have been gaining popularity. Dozens of local blues fans have been dropping by to have a beer and see their favourite players jam it out. From September to November, food and toy drives were conducted in partnership with St. Matthew's House. The community is becoming stronger as musicians and fans alike meet new friends who simply love the blues.

A key priority is to share and encourage the playing and enjoyment of blues music everywhere, so executive member Bill Watson took it upon himself to set up a live webcast of the jams in an effort to expand the audience even more. Watson's passion for photography keeps him doubly busy during the live performances.

The blues jams are free. Participants are encouraged to use the donation jar to help support future events. The HBS executive is excited about its mission. The next major steps will be incorporation and achieving charitable organization status.

THE RULES ARE CHANGING: ALAN CROSS

Internationally known broadcaster, writer and musicologist Alan Cross delivered the keynote address at the Hamilton Music Awards Industry Conference. With over 30 years in the music biz, Cross has produced programs like "The Ongoing History of New Music" and "Secret History of Rock." He works as an industry writer, public speaker, podcast creator for Geeks and Beats, and is deeply involved in exploring the present and future relationships between music, technology and social networking.

"The only form of media that is actually growing is mobile," said Cross. "What people are doing while they're driving is becoming more important. Cars are quickly becoming 'apps on wheels' and simply another device connected to the Internet.

Radio is not about distribution – AM or FM – it's about creating great content. We have to be open to delivering it in new ways to the digital generation. Will it be through the smartphone, the Internet, some type of new receiver? The audience wants what they want, when they want it, and on the device of their choice.

His advice on playing live: "Play, play, play for as many different people as possible. The audience will tell you the truth in 'real time.' If you suck you will know it. If you're good, you'll be encouraged. We pay artists to feel. We pay them to spill their guts. And that is very much worth something."

CUT FROM STEEL 2013

A YEAR IN REVIEW

By Biljana Djegovan

Photography **Amber Edgar (The Rest)**

MORE **CUT FROM STEEL** *HIGHLIGHTS*

HACHEY THE MOUTHPEACE

Jason Hachey is a beat maker, a singer, and most notably an amazing beat boxer. Hachey has been a part of the Hamilton music scene for a long time, but 2013 brought him to the masses. Hachey won the Much Music beat boxing championships earlier in the year and he showed the rest of the country what Hamilton's been known for a long time - Hachey rocks. His performance with the Hamilton Philharmonic Orchestra at Supercrawl was a unanimous festival weekend favourite.

PUCUMBER SASSQUASH FAMILY BAND

The best way to experience Pucumber Sassquash Family band is in the thick of a the crowd at a live show. Every person in this band is immensely talented and has contributed to Hamilton's music scene in some meaningful way over the past 10 years. They are loud. They are aggressive. They are poetic. They are Hamilton's best kept secret.

MOTHER TAREKA & THE GREEZY STEEZ

This monster of an ensemble band is quickly becoming a crowd favourite. The explosive hip hop collective is lead by rebel MC Mother Tareka who writes lyrics that make you want to get up and do something about our problems. The backing band is made up of members of some of Hamilton's finest: The Altobeelays, Haolin Munk with DJ LP. If Rage Against The Machine and The Roots had a love child - it would be named Mother Tareka and the Greezy Steez.

HIGH KITES

Made up of members of Cowlick, Terra Lightfoot band, Bruce Peninsula, and Blackburn, High Kites is one hell of a psych rock band. The musical mastery Dylan Hudecki, Steve McKay, and Dan Empringham bring to this project is unparalleled. As for the front man, Andy Richardson, you will have to attend a show to take in all of the charming magic. Put "seeing a High Kites show" at the top of your things to do list for 2014

I started Cut From Steel in January 2013 and it has been great capturing and documenting such a fantastic year of music.

A great year like 2013 is difficult to summarize, but there were a few standout moments that must be mentioned. We've always had fantastic hip hop producers and MCs in Hamilton, but 2013 was the year that the structure and support beams for the scene saw a major upgrade. The Steel Gold hip hop showcase was a monthly event that was instrumental in the strengthening of Hamilton's hip hop community and scene. Led by the passionate Sam Siva, this $5 event allowed bedroom DJs and first time rappers to get on stage and share their craft with a supportive crowd. The energy created when novice rappers get on stage and impress the crowd with their talent is amazing. Personally I loved attending every month and I was sad to see the event conclude in the fall. The hip hop community was left strong and connected, and many other people have stepped up to carry the torch. Promoters like In Tha Kut, and the Beat Binjaz worked tirelessly this year to bring exciting up and coming, as well as huge legendary hip hop acts to Hamilton.

One of the most rewarding experiences that Cut From Steel brought me this past year was the interview with The Rest. After 10 years as a band, The Rest parted ways this past June. Spending a few hours with the band as they prepared for their last two shows was truly special. Not only was The Rest a fantastic band made up of some seriously talented musicians and songwriters, they were incredibly nice and generous with their time. Hanging out with the band in their practice space while heavy fog and rain raged outside was a moment I won't soon forget. The last ever Hamilton show happened at the Dundas Valley Montessori school. Many guest musicians came up to play with the band and the place was packed with smiling faces.

Early this fall we had the second annual Johnny Cash tribute show put on by Lori Yates and the Nashville Rejects. The level of talent and musical mastery that the crowd witnessed at This Ain't Hollywood that night was astounding. Where else could you see the likes of Lori Yates, Lee Reed, Lou Molinaro, Sarah Beatty, Luke Bantham and Sue Lenoard share a stage? I look forward to many more years of this wonderful Johnny Cash tribute show.

And last, it would be difficult to highlight a year in music without mentioning the Supercrawl music and arts festival. Cut From Steel had access to interview a large number of both local and visiting bands and musicians. From local favourites like Young Rival and The Dirty Nil to headliners Wintersleep and Metz. We spoke to a lot of musicians. We also had press passes and were able to take some of the best photos featured on Cut From Steel to date. It turns out that standing a few feet away from a screaming punk band is a good way to take a memorable picture. Supercrawl's Sean Palmerston was kind enough to open a few doors for us and the coverage of the festival is something I'll be proud of for a long time. •

LOVE OF MUSIC
LORI YATES
By Kathryn Dunmore

"I DIDN'T KNOW WHAT I WAS TRYING TO ACHIEVE BUT I KNEW A WAY TO PLAY COUNTRY THAT HAD ENERGY, SPUNK AND APPEAL TO YOUNGER AUDIENCES."

Photography **Cormac Figgis**
Hair **Melissa Minnick**
Makeup **Stephaney Wojtania**

Performing country in Toronto at a time when it wasn't popular, but performing in Nashville when it was, Hamilton musician Lori Yates has always stepped outside of custom and made her musical career into one that has spanned decades.

Raised in Toronto, the veteran singer/songwriter was a country girl singing in punk clubs of the '80s in downtown Toronto. Not afraid of walking into new terrain, Yates' love of music and an evolutionary style was a driving pursuit, which garnered her substantial success, an ongoing career in music, and now a love of sharing her craft with others.

It all started with her love of Dolly Parton. Weaned on the renowned singer and others such as Tanya Tucker, and influenced by legendary bands such as Pink Floyd growing up, Yates created her own alternative sound as a young adult. "I had a burning desire to sing from a very early age," explained Yates. "I surrounded myself with music and my parents listened to a lot of music. I was drawn to country and had a love of singers like Dolly Parton early on. Although I was always interested in country, I wanted to put my own spin on it so I was also interested in cow punk."

She started performing live with her original new wave band The Last Resorts.

In the mid '80s, Yates wrangled her own alternative country/cow punk band Rang Tango in Toronto's Queen Street West music scene that produced bands such as Blue Rodeo and Cowboy Junkies. After a couple years performing with Rang Tango, Yates was picked up as a solo artist on Sony Nashville, and 'Can't Stop The Girl' was released worldwide in 1989. She toured with artists such as Big Sugar and Dwight Yoakam.

"I didn't know what I was trying to achieve but I knew a way to play country that had energy, spunk and appeal to younger audiences. I didn't see examples of that being done in Canada."

In Nashville, Yates spent several months co-writing with legendary writers such as Don Schiltz and Guy Clark before returning home. "It was a time when Nashville was the Mecca but when I was there, I saw what it was all about and it wasn't really what I wanted to do. Nashville thought I was really alternative and Toronto thought I was strange."

In 1993, she signed to Virgin Music Canada and released 'Breaking Point'. She toured with Blue Rodeo, Jann Arden and Faith Hill. Along the way, she was nominated for a Juno and CCMA awards. Her second album, 'Untogether', was released on Virgin Music Canada in 1996. "My first album was a country rock album and my second was a complete departure with trip hop; this was 1996 and I was the first female vocalist with loops behind me. Nobody was doing that, certainly not a country singer. It was refreshing for me, I needed a break from country and it's still one of my favourite records."

After working with major labels, Lori Yates worked independently and has released a total of six albums to date. She is now working on a new album set to be released spring 2014. She will tell you that despite having peaks and valleys in her career, her unwavering dedication to her creativity has defined her path as an artist.

Now, decades later, she still keeps things fresh by continually writing new music, performing live (which also includes a stand-up comedy routine) and even offering a songwriting workshop, called Creative Genius Songwriting Workshop, in Hamilton. "Writing new songs helps, playing with new musicians helps and different expressions, such as my songwriting workshop, are exciting," she noted. "I'm always trying new stuff. I still play with my band the Nashville Rejects and in December we're backing up a variety show with diverse and interesting artists." •

For more information, visit www.loriyates.com

A LEADER IN THE ART, SCIENCE AND BUSINESS OF MUSIC
MOHAWK COLLEGE APPLIED MUSIC PROGRAM

By James Tennant

"IN THE PAST, WE'D SEE STUDENTS WERE GREAT SONGWRITERS, BUT FOR THREE YEARS, THEY WERE ONLY PLAYING JAZZ. THAT'S A SOLID FOUNDATION, BUT NOT THE ONLY FOUNDATION."

Photography Ida Adamowicz

The music business has changed. Old structures have been broken down, reworked and built back up again – even if the facades are the same, the floor plans have changed. To succeed, people need new tools, new ways of thinking and new insights into what it means to be in the business of music. In some ways, a career in music today is similar to playing jazz. The best jazz players spend years honing their talents until they're nimble, able to take a chart and own it, to leap around an arrangement in ways that make you say man, "why didn't I think of that?" It's not just a skill, it's a way of thinking. It's a mindset.

Mohawk College has long been known for its Applied Music program. What people may not know is how that program has evolved along with the music industry. If you want to jump into the music business and own your place in it, the new music program at Mohawk will give you the skills and the mindset, with new curriculum and a new approach.

The three-year Applied Music diploma program, expanded from a two-year program, maintains an emphasis on music fundamentals even as it branches into new areas of study to address the world of music today.

The new computer lab, for example, houses the sort of software technology that is crucial for the business. At one time, purists may have scoffed, but it in now understood that software technology is merely a new tool to aid musicians with composition and arrangement. Used properly, it frees the imagination and assists creativity. The new curriculum teaches students to creatively apply these technologies to music production, songwriting, film scoring, advertising and other potential commercial applications. Students learn about acoustics, audio editing/manipulation, audio engineering, computer music composition, music broadcasting and distribution, soundtrack creation and more.

It can be difficult to reconcile the "art" of music with phrases such as "commercial application." Yet to build a music career, you can't deny music is also a commercial product. The music business employed countless full time musicians, composers, recording engineers, publicists and a myriad other professionals. At Mohawk, students are introduced to the fundamentals of entrepreneurial thinking, current trends in the music industry, and the concept of music and branding. Courses explore the music business as an industry in transition, while students reflect on that tension between music as art and commerce. They learn to understand and master the basic building blocks of the music industry: copyright, publishing, licensing, performing rights societies, touring, concert production and funding models.

Performance and music theory – fundamental core work like harmony and arranging – remain critical in the program. Yet even in these areas, Mohawk has expanded and deepened its prospectus to provide opportunities for students to explore creativity in new ways.

Darcy Hepner, the Applied Music Co-ordinator, is excited to see the emphasis on jazz expand into other areas. "In the past, we'd see students were great songwriters," says Hepner, "but for three years, they were only playing jazz. That's a solid foundation, but not the only foundation."

To that end, new courses in songwriting might focus on the popular music format, while courses on film scoring provide a truly practical application for something such as classical composition. Even with jazz, long a mainstay at Mohawk, new courses in improvi-

sation help students reach new heights of performance while learning an entirely different way to think about the creation of music.

On hand to teach all of these courses is a remarkable faculty of professionals (see sidebar). All have experience playing music across the continent, and between them, they've added exciting variety to the program. "We have many jazz ensembles," says Hepner, "but we've added ensembles based around Tower of Power, the Beatles, Latin music, Cuban music, bluegrass and plans for more, like an electronic/laptop ensemble."

Playing in ensembles is more than just rocking a cover of "Hey Jude." Even if it was just analyzing the song, learning the parts and memorizing the lyrics, that's still real-world application. Add to that the extremely real-world elements that come with it – dealing with monitors, sound engineers, maybe even a grumpy stage manager; publicizing the show, practicing, correcting technical issues, engaging and communicating with an audience in a legitimate music venue and being compared to the professional touring acts that appear there weekly – and suddenly the Beatles ensemble becomes the music equivalent of

a medical internship or a legal articling position. Students are active in the world in which they hope to thrive.

Students are also active on a local level, which is a boon for Hamilton music across the board. Timing is perfect for a new, elevated synergy between Mohawk students and the Hamilton music scene. Hamilton resembles a nascent Brooklyn, New York, with more performance and industry professionals now than ever before. Artists are relocating here, and post-secondary graduates are staying in Hamilton to pursue their career goals. Mohawk students are often part of the scene before they graduate, whether it's the Tower of Power horn ensemble playing alongside local indies at This Ain't Hollywood, or students ¬– on their own, outside of curriculum ¬– hosting open mic nights at local pubs or gigging regularly with their own acts. Mohawk students get real-world experience in Hamilton, and there are plenty of opportunities for them to forge music careers here.

Hamilton benefits greatly from its music scene. Music is part of our national, and even international, identity. It is part of our recent move toward economic prosperity. There's

even a Hamilton Music Strategy, aimed at fostering industry, musicians and consumers. Mohawk College's evolving Applied Music Program perfectly gels with the evolving artistic world of Hamilton.

"Mohawk's music program has expanded its curriculum to include the business of music and the new advancements in music technology," summarizes associate dean of Media and Entertainment, Ken Wallis. "These new initiatives will much better prepare Mohawk's students for the real world realities of the music industry"

The Applied Music Program at Mohawk College has evolved to keep pace with the world around it. Now more than ever it will assist students in developing their own musical personality, their own vision and direction. After graduation, they'll have the ability to look at this business in transition and say – metaphorically speaking – yeah, I can play that. I can make that my own. •

For information on the Applied Music Program please go to www.mohawkcollege.ca/media-entertainment-programs/applied-music-advanced-diploma

MOHAWK COLLEGE APPLIED MUSIC PROGRAM

By James Tennant

JAMSHED TUREL is a renowned violinist, academic scholar and film music composer/editor. He developed a music technology and filmscoring curriculum at Mohawk. His aims are twofold – giving students an opportunity to get orchestral experience and interact/perform with fellow classical musicians, and to familiarize students with cutting-edge technology in order to facilitate their music creation and further their careers.

"For me, technology was always a tool towards a creative purpose, but because I was comfortable with that tool, I could use it creatively. This is what I wanted to bring to the students: that level of comfort with technology so that they can use it in an inspired manner to further their career in music, whatever path it may take."

DARCY HEPNER has performed with legendary performers including B.B. King, Aretha Franklin, Sergio Mendes and Henry Mancini. He toured internationally with Blood Sweet & Tears, Buster Poindexter and Artie Shaw. Teaching is also a passion. Hepner was the founding department head of the Selkirk College Music Program in Nelson, BC and taught at the world famous Berklee College of Music in Boston.

"We aim to prepare students for the future. The technology component, the business component, they lead to that future. If you can provide a student with entrepreneurial skills, so they can sketch a vision of themselves and where they feel their passions could lead them, you're better equipping them to move forward."

PAT COLLINS, bass player and graduate of the Berklee College of Music in Boston, is an active performer on the Canadian jazz scene. He has performed with the likes of Oscar Peterson, Dizzy Gillespie and Diana Krall. Collins is also in demand as a clinician and teacher across the country.

"The heart and soul of what the Mohawk Music Program has always done hasn't changed, but we have become much more diverse with our curriculum as well as genres of music we teach and play. I hope the role of the Mohawk College Music Department continues to be an integral part of the Hamilton music community as our graduates continue to contribute invaluable contributions to the scene both locally, nationally and internationally."

ASTRID HEPNER is a musician, performer, teacher and professional with experience in media relations, advertising and management. After earning an MPA in her native Germany, she began a full time music career in New York City. She is the currently founder/chair of the Hamilton Music Collective and its "An Instrument For Every Child" campaign.

"Through the development of a comprehensive music business and arts entrepreneurship curriculum, we aim to equip our music students with the skills and tools they need to create sustainable careers, and to explore the vast opportunities inherent in a changing marketplace. We want our students to leave the program as accomplished artists and entrepreneurial thinkers, equipped with the skills necessary for a satisfying and sustainable career as an artist in the 21st Century."

TERRY BASOM holds a Bachelor and Master's degree in Music Education. As a freelance musician, Terry has worked with orchestras including the Hamilton, Niagara, London and Buffalo symphonies and has backed up countless performers such as Celine Dion, Tony Bennett and Aretha Franklin.

"In the last several years, the Music Department at Mohawk has introduced new curriculum and facility changes which have enhanced the program. Courses such as computer technology and jazz improvisation have been added with songwriting and recording yet to come. Mohawk music graduates are resourceful and innovative learners who have developed the skills to work in the competitive and increasingly demanding world of the music industry."

DUSTY MICALE is a songwriter, composer, arranger, keyboardist and producer whose work ranges from feature films, co-writing with superstars like Cyndi Lauper and playing keys for the likes of Gary US Bonds. He has a degree from Juilliard/New School New York City in classical composition. His background from songwriting and performing in rock bands to classical composition has given him a unique perspective.

"Wonderful things happen when boundaries are blurred and something new and original is born. In this spirit, Mohawk will be on the cutting edge. Commitment to technology combines with a firm grounding in music fundamentals providing for an exciting opportunity to develop a personal voice." •

CHASING THE WIND
GILLIAN NICOLA AND THE RADIO INTERFERENCE
By Jeffrey C. Martin

*Photography **Sarah Angela Ragelle***

Gillian Nicola is quickly establishing herself as one of the best voices in Hamilton. Her debut EP, Chasing the Wind by Gillian Nicola and the Radio Interference, netted her two Hamilton Music Award nominations, one for Alt/Country Recording of the Year and one for New Group/Artist of the Year.

"It's really an honour," Nicola said. "I didn't think we'd actually get nominated, but you know, it's really, really nice." Nicola started singing in her youth as a member of the Hamilton Children's Choir, and continued her passion for music into university.

Chasing the Wind was recorded with Dundas-based sound engineer Eric Persichini. Her brother, Benjamin Alexander, plays guitar and is used to playing a louder genre of music as part of the hardcore band Prophets. His unique musical perspective enhances the sound of the Radio Interference. Alexander says he appreciates the freedom Gillian Nicola and the Radio Interference allows him musically. "I've always want to play guitar solos, but I was always in a band that was sort of in-the-box," said Alexander.

Nicola says she's ready to continue making music. "I told [the band] that after we play our showcase at the Hamilton Music Awards, I have all-new music to teach them," she said. "It'll be nice to get some new stuff in our set." •

FUELING THE CITY'S MUSIC SCENE
HAMILTON MUSIC STRATEGY
By Jeffrey C. Martin

On the heels of the Ontario government's Live Music Strategy, launched in early 2013 to showcase the industry globally with a $45 million investment fund, the City of Hamilton is moving in sync with its own music directive.

To advance the music sector of Hamilton's creative industries and to align with the provincial initiative, City of Hamilton staff were directed by City Council at its meeting in May 2013 to "establish a music working group and report back on a Hamilton Music Strategy, and the possibility of establishing a Hamilton Music Office."

The directive recognizes Hamilton's deep-rooted and vibrant music scene, and the importance for the city to establish itself as a key music destination for musicians, music industry players, and music tourists. Council also directed staff to connect with the Canadian Academy of Recording Arts and Sciences (CARAS), Global Spectrum Hamilton and CTV in an effort to host – for the sixth time – the next available Juno Awards at Copps Coliseum.

Jackie Norton of Hamilton's Culture and Tourism Division, assisted in the establishment of the volunteer working group from across the local music community. "The music community in Hamilton came forward immediately to participate in the discussions around the provincial Live Music initiative and related initiatives in Hamilton," said Norton. "These are fabulous, energetic people, ready to get to work to support the community. We quickly established a working group and identified priorities for a music strategy."

The working group's final document covers a range of issues, from music and economic development and a review of Hamilton's music scene and community, to government music Initiatives, other music cities, and more. It also reflects the City's recently adopted Cultural Plan 2013 (Transforming Hamilton Through Culture), as well as Hamilton's Economic Development Strategy (2010–2015) which defines music as encompassing the six key elements: music retail, music groups, artists and companies, sound recording companies, art instruction (music education), promoters (presenters) of music, and performing arts facilities (music). It will be presented to Council in late 2013 or early 2014. "Music has always been such a major component of this city's cultural fabric and we're very excited about shining a brighter light on the abundance of great talent here."

There are four funding streams within the new Ontario Music Fund, supporting both not-for-profit and for-profit companies and organizations. These four categories include: Music Company Development Fund, Music Industry Development Fund, Music Futures Fund, and the Live Music Fund (deadlines vary so check the web site for details: http://www.omdc.on.ca/music/the_ontario_music_fund/music_industry_development.htm. Municipalities are not eligible to apply but will be able to work with any application as a secondary partner.

Hamilton's Music Strategy will play a pivotal role in forging this city's part in "positioning Ontario as a premier global destination for live music and music tourism through the province's international marketing initiatives." Imagination and determination to access the provincial funds could place Hamilton musicians and music venues into a more prominent place within Ontario's regional, national and international tourism efforts.

Like other established music cities – Seattle, Portland, Austin, Birmingham, Glasgow and Brooklyn NY – all eyes will be on how the music strategy supports and grows Hamilton's vibrant and eclectic music scene. •

NO MORE WAITING FOR
DANIELLE BEAUDIN
By David Simpson

'MY DAD IS A YOUNG FREE SPIRIT AND A DREAMER,
I GUESS THAT'S WHERE I GET IT FROM."

Photography **Cormac Figgis**

Danielle Beaudin knew in grade 9, growing up on the Hamilton Mountain, that she wanted to be a rock-and-roll singer. When she should have been studying for school exams, Beaudin was playing her guitar, fiddling with a basic multi-track recorder, and writing songs.

In Grade 12, she arranged her own co-op placement at Westmoreland Studios, which was run by Carl Jennings of the local band Freedom Train. She has been working there ever since and, during what little downtime there has been has been recorded with Jennings as producer of her first album, "Wait for Your Love." She launched her new album party in October 2013 at Hamilton's This Ain't Hollywood.

The nine songs on the album were, to varying degrees, six years in the making. It takes time and money to record, mix, and master a song. The final product is the result of a lot of hard work and sacrifice – dining on Kraft Dinner instead of caviar.

Beaudin wrote all the songs, although she credits Jennings on all of them for the contributions he made in helping to challenge her and to shape the song arrangements and sound quality. A few tunes were written in the studio, and very much influenced by Carl's creative ideas. "Carl and I have a good relationship in the studio," said Beaudin. "We play a tennis match of sorts, bouncing ideas back and forth. I can't praise Carl enough for everything he did for these new songs, and

can definitely say some of these tunes are a 50-50 writing credit."

Helping out at a recording studio has also taught her a lot – and she has been involved in engineering and contributing backing vocals on many projects along the way.

A lot of songs on the album have a classic sound and feel – driven by electric guitar, catchy choruses and layered harmonies. Her influences include The Beatles, Fleetwood Mac, Joni Mitchell, Neil Young, and other classic rock acts – music that was frankly before her time. She credits her father for some of her musical tastes. He was a DJ and, while he encouraged his children to listen to contemporary music, he loved the old stuff and has shared his collection of vinyl LPs with his daughter.

Beaudin says that her dad loves music and gets out to see bands two or three times a week – more than she does. Sometimes she'll get a text from friends saying that they're hanging out at a live show with her dad. "My dad is a young, free spirit and a dreamer," she said. "I guess that's where I get it from. He always encouraged both my actor brother and I to do what we love, to find our passion and to follow where it leads. My mom is also amazing and supportive of my goals – she's my rock and keeps me sane when I feel like my world gets too crazy, which it often does."

Beaudin has videos for three of the songs

posted on her website. The earliest video, "Little Bird," edits together grainy, old home movies of her father and his siblings. "Sun Will Shine," with its bright chorus, features some shots of her on figure skates – something she still teaches part-time. Miz Monday put this video together for Beaudin. Her latest video is the new album's title song " Wait For Your Love" and features artful camera angles with Beaudin in various Hamilton settings. March Mercanti helped bring it to life.

Working at Westmoreland, with its busy recording schedule, Beaudin has made the acquaintance of many talented musicians along the way. Musicians who helped on her album have experience playing with The Trews, City and Colour, David Wilcox and other established Canadian bands. Her principal performing partner is Tim Allard, who handles drums, keyboards and guitar with great skill.

Danielle has been playing live for years, building a fan base at clubs in Hamilton, Brantford, Stoney Creek, Burlington, and beyond. She also has a friend with a connection to the BBC in England – which she hopes will get her some airplay across the big pond. And in today's Internet-driven world, a singer/songwriter can make a breakthrough almost anywhere with a lot of talent and a little luck. Let's hope so for Beaudin. ●

This article was first printed in the McMaster Silhouette. Used with permission.

BEYOND THE CORNERS OF KING AND JAMES
DEEP ROOTS: HAMILTON'S MUSIC LEGACY

By Jeffrey C. Martin

"IT WAS THE SUMMER OF '57 WHEN HAROLD KUDLATS BOOKED CONWAY TWITTY INTO THE FLAMINGO LOUNGE ON MACNAB STREET. TWITTY STAYED IN HAMILTON FOR THE NEXT FEW MONTHS AND CO-WROTE WITH HIS DRUMMER JACK NANCE, 'IT'S ONLY MAKE BELIEVE' IN BETWEEN SETS AT THE FLAMINGO."

An impressive roster of many of Canada's acclaimed musicians, songwriters and producers, as well as some very distinguished visiting contemporaries, have called Hamilton and Hamilton's music scene "home." While many people think of Hamilton's music scene in contemporary terms, this ambitious working class city established itself as a vibrant music community long before the rise of blues, folk, jazz or rock 'n' roll. Hamilton's reputation as an important centre of music, and a city of music "firsts" was founded long ago in the late 19th Century.

THE BEGINNINGS
Hamilton's music legacy traces back to the Hamilton Musical Institute, which was founded in 1888 by D.J. O'Brien and renamed the Hamilton College of Music in 1899. According to Hamilton Public Library history archives, "In 1904, the Conservatory was incorporated and moved to James Street South. It opened its doors the following spring. The Conservatory thrived for the next 60 years. Student enrolment expanded and branches opened across Hamilton and southern Ontario. The Conservatory is just one of many milestones strengthening Hamilton's historical reputation as an important regional centre for music."

George Fenwick, a writer, musician and composer, and son of Scottish soprano Maggie Barr, taught music in Hamilton for 37 years and became the first provincial music supervisor – director of music for the Ontario Department of Education in 1935. Fenwick held this position for 34 years, advancing the cause of music through textbooks, radio broadcasts, inspectoral visits and promotion of competitions and festivals.

In "Some Musical Memories, 1964 Wentworth Bygones, No. 6" (Head-of-the-Lake Historical Society), Fenwick wrote: "Hamilton has a rich history of musical performance from its earliest days with many concerts, festivals and pantomimes featuring local talent as well as guest musicians and singers. In the early 19th century, Hamilton had an abundance of good music and good musicians but as the city was 'almost entirely populated by people from the British Isles, where a singing tradition always has been strong,' a lot of the music presented was of a vocal and choral nature."

MID-CENTURY 'S COMING OF AGE
In 1949, the Hamilton Philharmonic Orchestra (HPO) was founded. Olive Short, mother of comedian/actor Martin Short, was not only a former HPO concertmaster, but also the first female concertmaster in North America. Twenty years after its founding, the HPO went from amateur ensemble to professional orchestra. With great fervor, energy, and inventive performances, Boris Brott completely changed the orchestra's profile and stature. One of his "inventive" performances was actually held in Dofasco's steel mills. Under Brott's leadership, attendance at HPO concerts soared – from 23,000 to 225,000.

Harold Kudlats, uncle of SCTV alumni, actor/comedian Eugene Levy, was Canada's influential and illustrious music promoter and talent agent. After managing the long gone Hamilton Forum on Barton Street East, he went on to promote the biggest names of the era – Duke Ellington, Louis Armstrong, Jack Benny, Benny Goodman, Tommy Dorsey, Count Basie, Nat King Cole, among many others. In 1950, Kudlats became an agent and opened the Harold Kudlats Agency at the Royal Connaught Hotel. In the coming decade, he would help make music history.

A ROOTS TRADITION…
BLUES, COUNTRY AND FOLK MUSIC
During the last half of the 20th century, and into the first decade of the 21st century, Hamilton served as an incubator for some of Canada's best musical talent – beginning with the arrival of rockabilly and U.S. expatriates Conway Twitty and Ronnie Hawkins on to Hamilton's music scene in the late '50s.

It was the summer of '57 when Harold Kudlats booked Harold Lloyd Jenkins (aka Conway Twitty) into the downtown Flamingo Lounge on MacNab Street. Twitty stayed in Hamilton for a few months and co-wrote with his drummer Jack Nance, "It's Only Make Believe" in between sets at the Flamingo in 1958. By year-end, the record was number one in the U.S. and the U.K., as well as 21 other countries – the first of nine top 40 hits for Twitty. The following year, Kudlats brought Ronnie Hawkins to Canada. Ronnie and the Hawks first played at Hamilton's Golden Rail on King Street East. This music "first" laid the foundation for what eventually would become one of pop music and Canada's greatest and most influential groups, The Band.

>>>

<<< In the 1960s, it was the ascendancy of blues legends King Biscuit Boy (Richard Newell) and Jackie Washington, and career launch of R&B/soul/blues musician Harrison Kennedy, followed by the national and international impact of Crowbar, Ian Thomas, punk rockers Teenage Head and renown producer Daniel Lanois in the '70s and '80s. And while the music industry was beginning its gradual "implosion" as a result of digital technology, the Internet and corporate greed, Hamilton's indie music scene was literally exploding across all music genres in the 1990s and 2000s.

CITY OF MUSIC

Today, Hamilton's eclectic regional music scene is getting more recognition and renewed critical attention much like the vibrant music scenes that evolved in Birmingham, Glasgow, Brooklyn, Portland, Seattle and Austin.

The breadth of Hamilton's music diversity and its significance is evident when you consider the hundreds of established musicians, artists, bands, musical ensembles and professionals that have been recognized by city's own annual mini-Junos event, the Hamilton Music Awards. There is a definite buzz humming throughout this musically ambitious city. Hamilton's music and arts communities have become magnets for young musicians and artists from Toronto and other parts of southern Ontario. History has shown us that for both homegrown and visiting "musicians-in-residence" alike, the city of Hamilton has been not only a great place to live, but also a great place to write, record and play live music. ●

Previous page left
Olive Short
(Courtesy of The Hamilton Spectator)

Previous page right
Harrison Kennedy
Photography **Cormac Figgis**

This page clockwise from top left
Ian Thomas; Teenage Head; Jackie Washington *(left)* **and Brian Griffith** *(right)*
Photography **Jimmy Katz**
(Courtesy of Hamilton Music Collective)

www.porcelainrecords.com

hamilton, ontario

AWARD WINNING ART DIRECTOR

HPO HAMILTON
PHILHARMONIC
ORCHESTRA

Redeeming. Enriching. Classic. Captivating.

Music
Lives
Here

hpo.org

SWITCHESDESIGN
CORMAC FIGGIS

c 289 808 3064
e cormacfiggis@gmail.com

d www.switchesdesign.com

LIGHTS, CAMERA, ACTION!
FUNDING YOUR OWN MUSIC VIDEO

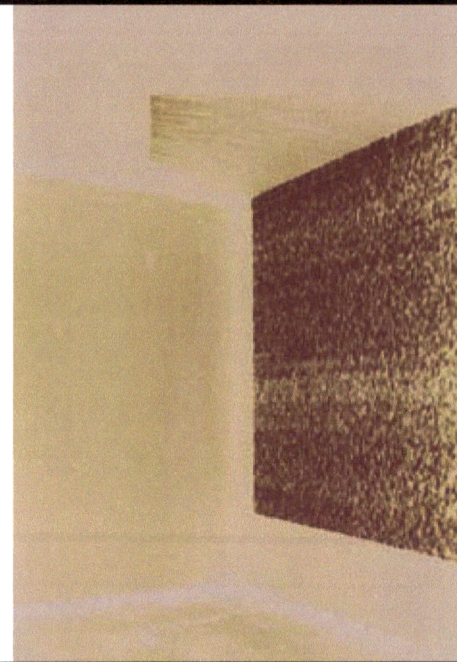

"WHAT MANY DON'T REALIZE IS THAT THERE ARE ALREADY MANY FINANCIAL RESOURCES AVAILABLE TO LOCAL MUSICIANS SPECIFICALLY DESIGNED FOR VIDEO PRODUCTION."

Do you want to bring more fans out to your shows, sell more tracks on iTunes, or simply get more gigs? In today's social media-centric world, there's no better way to promote yourself and your music than with a YouTube video.

The ultimate goal for any independent musician, and the hardest to achieve, is for a video to "go viral" on the Internet, propagating itself first among existing fans (Twitter/Facebook followers and friends) and ideally expanding beyond regional borders. For a video to be considered "share worthy," it needs to have good sound and video quality, entice an emotional connection with the viewer, and most importantly, be unique. Producing such a video requires planning, time and usually some money. What many don't realize is that there are already many financial resources available to local musicians specifically designed for video production. Applying for these grants can be a daunting task, but your chances are best if you work with an experienced and reputable production company.

"There are many music video and electronic press kit (EPK) funding sources available to local artists, such as MuchFACT, FACTOR and BAND TOGETHER," said Tim Dashwood,

founder of Hamilton-based 11 Motion Pictures (11motionpictures.com). "The trickiest part of applying for these grants is preparing a first-class creative pitch with an appropriate budget proposal. We've been doing it for almost 15 years now, and in that time we've managed to come up with the ideal recipe for video grant approvals."

MuchMusic's MuchFACT (muchfact.ca) will fund music videos, web productions, EPKs and viral videos. MuchFACT will cover 50 per cent of the production budget, but each program has a maximum amount they will fund: video $25,000, web production $3,500, EPK $3,500 and viral $3,500.

FACTOR's video program (www.factor.ca/ourprograms/video) helps finance original music videos that support qualifying sound recordings by Canadian artists. FACTOR will kick in up to 75 per cent of eligible costs to a maximum of $5,000 (Intermediate Level) or $20,000 (Advanced Level.)

BAND TOGETHER is an initiative of Hamilton-based arts service organization CoBALT Connects (cobaltconnects.ca). It is a non-profit that facilitates a connection between musicians and media artists to work together as

they create music videos that help each partner reach their creative goals. Last year they provided funds to four local artists.

"As someone who was involved with one of the Band Together videos, it was amazing to see so much creativity with a relatively small budget," said local musician/filmmaker Nathan Fleet. "When artists work together with a common goal in mind, it's amazing what they can accomplish."

Of course there are always ways to raise funds for your video project outside of the grant system by using Kickstarter, Indiegogo or even a Paypal "donate" button on your website. "We can produce top-notch performance videos for as little as $500, live multi-camera shows for $5,000, or sophisticated concept videos for as much as $25,000," said Dashwood. "It really just boils down to what best serves the creative intentions of the artist. For example, Burlington's Walk Off The Earth had an amazing viral success with a single-shot video of the five of them playing one guitar. It was simple yet very creative and was definitely social media 'share-worthy.'" •

For more information visit
www.11MotionPictures.com

MUSIC VIDEOS   EPKS   LIVE SHOWS   FILMS   11MotionPictures.com

FOR THE RECORD
HAMILTON'S
RECORD STORES

HAMMER CITY RECORDS

IIt's no secret that some of the most important early and influential punk music has its roots in Hamilton, and those bands found refuge in many of the local record shops. Teenage Head and later the Forgotten Rebels hung out at Star Records at the corner of King and James. Simply Saucer called Bob Moody's record bar on John Street one of their "homes away from home."

Record stores are more than places to buy music. They play a key role in any scene by giving musicians and fans a place to connect outside of venues, to spread news about upcoming gigs and share new music. Hammer City Records opened three years ago with an aim to provide punk, metal and hardcore vinyl direct to local fans. "From our tiny basement just off James Street North, I couldn't foresee just how the local scene would explode," said owner Craig Caron.

Caron has seen bands visit the store and then heard their sounds change in relation to their vinyl selections. After-hours space for merchandise runs, promo shoots and spending time listening to music with patrons are some of his favourite aspects of the store.

"Since the shop opened, the focus of our longstanding record label, Schizophrenic Records, has shifted from international bands to highlighting local music with releases from TV Freaks, Born Wrong, Chris Houston, Sailboats Are White, Snake Charmer and local compilations. Our monthly all-ages matinée show is also a great way to connect with younger bands and fans in the area," Caron continued.

Punk rock has always been about breaking down barriers and building a community. "We look forward to seeing your band on stage," said Caron. "Reading your fanzine or checking out your artwork and hope to see you at Hammer City Records – down the alley and in the pit where punk belongs. You are the scene." •

RAISING THE ROOF DR DISC

Dr. Disc is a music store that has been thriving and surviving in downtown Hamilton since 1991. The "Raise the Roof" concert series was initiated in 2011 to not only recognize and highlight some of the best bands in Hamilton and surrounding area, but also to give back to the local community for its valued and continued support.

Each "Raise the Roof" session takes place on the lower rear roof outside the store at 20 Wilson Street (weather permitting) and coincides with Art Crawl Friday, the second Friday of every month. These free sessions are open to the public, and commence in May and continue through October.

RAISE THE ROOF CONCERTS
FEATURE only local, independent musical artists of all genres and expose them to as widespread audience as possible.
GENERATE product sales for each band who are encouraged bring down and sell any recordings they may have.
INCREASE awareness of and highlight the diversity and vitality of the independent Hamilton music scene

ENCOURAGE the public to come to downtown Hamilton to experience all that it has to offer.

Featured acts that have performed include a veritable who's who in Hamilton and area music: Jessy Lanza, Harlan Pepper, the Dinner Belles, Ascot Royals, the Monarch Project, Dawn and Marra, Ginger St. James, the Dirty Nil, Hachey the MouthPeace, All About Maggie, New Hands, Harrison Kennedy and many others too numerous to mention.

This concert series has become so popular that the September session has been integrated in with Supercrawl, Hamilton's largest outdoor festival. Dr. Disc now hosts a separate stage featuring high profile, hand-picked local acts. Bands are now being booked for 2014 and all interested parties may contact Mark Furukawa via email (drdiscinc@bell-net.ca) for more information. Note that to be considered, the band (or the majority of its members) must be from Hamilton or surrounding area, and preference is given to artists that have finished recordings. •

CRASH LANDING IN THE EAST END

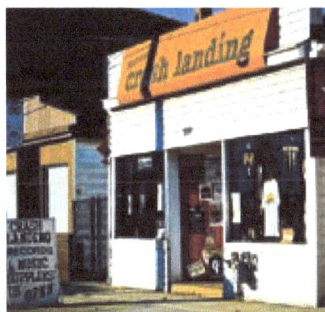

Located at 1189 Cannon Street East, steps away from the Corner of Ottawa and Cannon, is Crash Landing Music. In a time when "ma and pa" music stores are going out of business, Crash Landing continues to grow and expand. Store-owners are husband-and-wife team Chris "Crash" and Suzanne Kirkwood. Crash is a known character with 30 years of ongoing activity in Hamilton's punk scene. He plays guitar with Steeltown Spoilers (album awaiting release) and the Rezentments.

The shop proudly stocks an exclusive collection of rock and punk t-shirts along with eclectic, sometimes rare, vintage music equipment and music biz paraphernalia.

"We have a great selection of vintage collectible vinyl records and CDs," said Crash. "Certain items are taken on consignment. We've new stock coming in daily, lots of new rock, punk, blues, metal and country t-shirts. And we also sell D'Addario strings and music supplies, picks, sticks, Evans skins, tuners, straps and more."

The shop will be undergoing some renovations in the new year to improve the floor and record bins.

Kirkwood sums it all up: "Chris and I met in 1980 in the Hamilton punk scene and dated for three years. We were reunited in 2005 and set up Crash Landing a year later. We were mature enough now to realize how much Hamilton and its music meant to us, so we opened up our first shop on Ottawa street. We attend the monthly Slamfest shows downtown because we like to keep in touch with the scene. We support the Hamilton music and arts community by advertising shows and distributing gig flyers to our customers. We were both born and raised in Hamilton, and we love it." •

TWENTY FIVE YEARS OF
FREEDOM TRAIN
By Kathryn Dunmore

"I HOPE WE INSPIRE PEOPLE TO KEEP GOING. IF YOU PUT A BAND TOGETHER, PLAY SONGS YOU LOVE AND PLAY THEM WELL, YOU CAN DO IT."

*Photography **Dimo Safari***

With 2014 marking its 25th anniversary, Hamilton band Freedom Train knows the right track to independent success.

Formed by Carl Jennings as vocalist and bass guitarist, Ed Mitchell as guitarist and Tim Jennings as vocalist and drummer, the power trio features a four octave vocal range covering a myriad of styles from great artists and bands.

The band, performing throughout southern Ontario, plays an average of 200 shows a year and has done so for almost a quarter of a century.

"We play three to four nights a week minimum and it's been that way for 24 years," said Carl Jennings. "We can't believe it ourselves that we still enjoy it as much as we do. We genuinely feel lucky to do what we do. We are lucky to have this as our job as we really do love it."

Since 1989, Freedom Train has been performing classic songs and band favourites, working up to a repertoire of several hundred songs.

"Our one rule as a band is that all three of us have to agree on the song," noted Jennings. "We all have to like it and feel comfortable playing it. We also do care that we do the songs well. We perform songs by great artists and we have respect for that and a need to play them well. I think people respond to that."

People have responded well, ensuring Freedom Train performs at least three nights a week, often saving Saturday nights for special events.

"Being a part of so many special events, like birthdays, weddings, surprise parties and company successes is very rewarding. It has this energy of celebration. We get to play so many gigs based around positive energy that it makes it easy for us to be up and on."

The band spent the summer performing in festivals such as the Waterdown Rib Fest with special guest Dave Rave joining the band to sing classic Teenage Head songs, as well as the Burlington Rib Fest, Canada's largest Rib Fest, in September.

Playing special events, clubs and fundraisers routinely, Freedom Train has also taken the stage in venues such as Hamilton Place and Toronto's Massey Hall.

"We've done all kinds of crazy gigs and seen a lot of craziness over the years," Jennings said, recalling one event at a nudist music festival. "We have so many great stories."

Next year, the band plans to celebrate its quarter century in style with fellow musicians helping in the festivities.

A local musician, Chris Jupp, started Operation: 25 Years of Freedom Train on Facebook where he is gearing up to mark the occasion with an event in Burlington as well as collecting photographs from over the years for a scrapbook.

Jennings said other events will also be added to celebrate this milestone.

"I hope we inspire people to keep going," said Jennings. "If you put a band together, play songs you love and play them well, you can do it."

The band has become so well honed over the years that the band members only get together a couple of times a year to work out more complex songs, usually working a new song into its set in the sound check before the show.

The love of music and quality songs is what fuels these three musicians in performing time and again.

"At the end of the day, we're still playing our instruments and singing songs with as much passion as if they were our own anyway." •
View upcoming dates for Freedom Train at www.freedomtrain.ca.

LOCAL LUMINARIES SPICE UP
HARVEST PICNIC
By Tom Shea

The Greenbelt Harvest Picnic is always a good time. When your starting premise is 12 hours of great live music, you can't go wrong. But when you put that music in a lush and lovely conservation area, and when you tie it in with local farmers, artists, food vendors, and social activists, it's a recipe for locavore nirvana.

The 2013 "picnic" held true to form. Sure, there were the obligatory big-name ringers: a less-than-stellar Gordon Lightfoot and a tran-scendently beautiful Emmylou Harris topped the bill, not to mention a spellbinding set from event co-founder Daniel Lanois himself. There was also a wide range of national and international indie and folk talent, including Basia Bulat, Rocco DeLuca, the (sort-of-local) superduo Whitehorse, and the delightfully quirky Martha Wainwright.

But the focus was right where it was supposed to be – squarely on homegrown talent.

While local farmers hawked their strawberries, cherry tomatoes, concord grapes and kale chips, the main stage resounded with the music of such diverse and talented local luminaries as Terra Lightfoot, Derek Miller, Dawn & Marra, Ohnia:kara and Brian Griffith. Not to mention the particularly great sets by a rambunctious Harlan Pepper and Hamilton's own genuine rock 'n' rollers, the Arkells. •

Clockwise from top left
Emmylou Harris *(far right)* **with Sandrine** *(far left)* **and Malcolm Burn** *(centre)*; *(left to right)* **Trixie Whitley, Emmylou and Basia Bulat; Daniel Lanois; Harrison Kennedy; Brian Griffith** *(left)* **and Trevor O' Dowd** *(right)*; **Gordon Lightfoot.**

Photography **Cormac Figgis**

A GREAT DAY IN HAMILTON

HARRISON KENNEDY
FUNDRAISER

Thanks to Bill Watson, the man with the lens, for capturing this special moment. Think of it as a highly concentrated drop in Hamilton's big bucket of talent! The occasion was a fundraiser for Harrison Kennedy at 'This Ain't Hollywood' just across the street from the LIUNA Station location pictured here. Expressing his gratitude, Kennedy testified, "Prostate cancer is a silent killer. You guys killed me that day."

Front row left to right: Danny Lockwood, Darren Lachance, Sean O'Grady (crouching), Jacob Moon, Neil Nickafor, Harrison Kennedy, Steve Strongman, Paul Intson, Frank Koren, Kim Koren, Donna Panchezak, Lily Sazz, Tiffany Thompson. *Middle row left to right:* Benny Farrugia, Larry Murphy, Dave King, Guitar Mikey McMillan, Ian Thomas, Chris Chambers, Mark LaForme, Paul Panchezak, Rob Gellner, Alex MacDougall, Greg Smith, Ron Copple. *Back row left to right:* Adam Ostrosser, Mike Eastman, Sal Roselli, Brian Griffith, Steve Collett, Carl Jennings, Kevin McLean, Brian Rutherford, Tim Tickner, Larry Feudo, Phil (Farley) Byrne, Peter McFarland, Kim Campanero, Jay Burr, Bob Kirkpatrick. *Photography Bill Watson*

25

LUKE CUMMINS' PICKS
UNDERGROUND & INDIE
ILLITRY

Illitry make electro-organic music. If you're not sure what that means, I was a bit baffled too. After seeing them several times their brand of electronic sound became easily understood and captivating. Illitry wields sampled sounds and loops masterfully, filling the space with warm tones and thick effects. Over the past year or so they've added in a full percussion section, giving their thick sound yet another move-inducing power. Singer Troy Witherow is a man possessed behind his synths. His body jolts and thrashes with each tone engaged and his voice keeps some of the lighter noises from floating away. Chester Edington simultaneously lays down gorgeous sheets with the guitar and has even added to the percussive onslaught during live jam sessions.

Which leads to Illitry's great-est advancement. They've been in the studio for quite some time now preparing their debut album. From the teases they've given to fans, including the fantastic single "Goshen", they're keen to take their time and ensure that each layer and note is perfectly arranged. Sometimes a lengthy studio stay can signal trouble, but from their recent showings at Supercrawl and This Ain't Hollywood, the extended time has improved their connection and ability. The jams they've been integrating into their performances hint at a band that are primed to share that brand of humanizing, yet not altogether human music they initially set out to create, albeit with a more explosive component that was discovered along the way. Look for the LP early 2014. •
www.illitry.com

DARK MEAN

One of Hamilton's hidden gems, while the gents of Dark Mean continue to gather new fans worldwide (some two years after the release of their excellent self-titled debut), their sparse live appearances have kept them a secret in our hometown. Writer/director Stephen Chbosky (The Perks of Being a Wallflower, Jericho) recently tweeted his appreciation for their song "Lullaby" so they are definitely on some interesting radars. With grace and honesty, Dark Mean create mosaics of insight and infinitely pleasing rhythms. They're putting the finishing touches on an EP that will further expose their masterful way of sharing deeply personal stories in a universal way, inviting listeners to revel in the mysteries of love and loss. Stay really tuned. •
www.darkmean.com

BLACK BARON

Giving some of the most enigmatic local vibe thrashers a run for their money (see: WTCHS), Black Baron has seven songs on their bandcamp site but very little in the way of an online presence. From behind a wall the four muted songs of their cassette, Divine Chains, chug along with blurry guitars and smeared percussion. Some call it post-punk but it might be post-everything. A friend tried describing them to me before I listened and he mentioned Joy Division. That's about right. It's as if Ian Curtis is calling us on a phone from where ever he went when he left us, and all of the dimensions between are providing mysterious, distorted layers. Who wouldn't want to take that call? •
blackbaron.bandcamp.com

SCOTT ORR

The DIY label Other Songs Music Co. has released some inspired and beautiful music over the years. Of those fine releases, Scott Orr has contributed greatly. His newest collection, A Long Life, is surely his most engaging, though. These 10 songs are completely capturing and fully expose Orr's ability to evoke a feeling. Strings, keys and voices comfort you with the ambiguous sadness that only nostalgia can bring. A Long Life is available with its beautiful cover art in cassette, compact disc and vinyl formats. Grab the cassette for a bonus track and the vinyl for the warm sound only it can bring (and a nifty poster of the album art too). •
www.scott-orr.com

TV FREAKS

An opener like "Rewind" is nothing short of punk genius. As an introduction track on their newest album, TWO, it harnesses all of the good things about punk without feeling contrived. Like the rest of the record, "Rewind" is a concise and wild ride. Furious pacing and stabbing guitars immediately rip you out of any state you were in before pressing play. Things are balanced just enough for you to make out every screeching word Dave O'Connor spews, making it really easy to rip your own vocal chords apart singing along. And sing you will, in the same urgent manner that permeates from every second of TWO (it's near impossible not to). Make sure you have some lozenges handy for the next day though. •
televisionfreaks.blogspot.ca/

Clockwise from top
The Trailblazers *(left to right)* **Lily Sazz, Joe Lomano, Melanie Jean, Alex MacDougall and Gerry Gregg;** *Shadows Taking Over* by **Alex MacDougall;** *Beyond the Green Door* by **Alex MacDougall**

SOUL OF A GENERATION
ALEX MACDOUGALL:
A MEMOIR
By Kevin Barber

"GIGGING WITH HAMILTON LEGENDS SUCH AS RICHARD NEWELL (KING BISCUIT BOY), KELLY JAY, RAY MATERICK AND HARRISON KENNEDY, MACDOUGALL WAS FRONT AND CENTRE DURING THE GOLDEN YEARS OF CANADIAN MUSIC."

JANUARY 22, 1951 - JULY 19, 2013

The world lost not only a great musician in Alex MacDougall, but also someone who embodied the very soul of a generation who, valued music as a genuine life force.

Brought to the former Steel City by Reg Titian and soon playing with Rita Chiarelli, the Truro, Nova Scotia native hailed from a musical family where the guitar was revered as more than a musical instrument, it was an instrument of change. Gigging with Hamilton legends such as Richard Newell (King Biscuit Boy), Kelly Jay, Ray Materick and Harrison Kennedy, MacDougall was front and centre during the golden years of Canadian music. Years of hard work and dedication to his craft made Alex a sought after stage and session player for many, and was a seminal member of some great local groups such as The Trailblazers and Groove Corporation.

Curious and gifted, Alex was soon recognized as an engineer and producer, helping to create magic that will be treasured for eternity. Life as a full time musician is 'hard scrabble' and not often kind to those who choose this path. When Alex used his affinity for technology and computers to obtain his Microsoft certification, his subsequent work at Employment Hamilton allowed him to help some of the most vulnerable citizens of this city as IT co-ordinator while remaining active in the music community. Alex treasured this role, as he was able to see daily, the results of his ongoing efforts.

Low key and soft spoken, Alex managed to remain positive and embraced the future even during the dark days that weigh on us all. As a fairly private person, Alex honed the ability to make conversations centre around the other person, and in doing so, become truly connected on another level. I was often left quite impressed at his ability to remember the names of so many people at a show, and that he would make introductions on a regular basis, leading to many lifetime relationships.

It is said of musicians that they only really live when they play. I have no doubt that as the music flowed through him, Alex was in his element – perhaps the only times he felt completely at ease and in control. Thankfully, we have a lifetime of recordings to remember Alex MacDougall, an archival collection with that rare blend of precision and feel that elude so many. Listen to his tasty riffs, soaring solos and verve fuelled chops and you will not only hear, but actually feel the essence of his soul. Professional to the core, no recording ever left his hands without receiving all he could do to make it the best. He made so many of us better, and he will be missed every day. ●

DIGITAL DIY: ONLINE TOOLKITS FOR MUSICIANS GETTING YOUR MUSIC KNOWN
By Kathleen Farley

ABOUT DOMAIN NAMES AND WEB HOSTING
yourband.com/.ca

You've set up your social media presence: Facebook, Twitter, YouTube. Check. You may even have your own website, either through a hosted service (wordpress.com, blogger.com) or as a self-hosted website on your own shared web hosting plan.

Why stop there? Here are 10 free online tools to take your digital presence to the next level.

PAYMENT GATEWAYS *(MAKE IT EASY TO PURCHASE YOUR MUSIC)*

Chances are, you'll need to send or receive money online for you or your band at some point. If you don't already have a PayPal account, it's a good idea to set one up. PayPal has become the de facto standard for internet payments worldwide. *www.paypal.com*

Wouldn't it be great to accept credit cards in person, or at your merch table? Sign up for a free Square account and get a free credit card reader to plug into your iOS or Android device. *www.squareup.com/ca*

SALES PORTALS *(PROMOTE YOUR SHOWS AND RELEASES)*

Why not presell tickets to your next gig? Use Guestlist to set up an event and sell tickets online. Guestlist provides a polished experience for your fans, including gorgeous automated emails, printable tickets, and mobile support. *www.guestlistapp.com*

When it comes to selling music and merchandise online, it's hard to beat Bandcamp. Embed their customizable music player on your website, or use the Bandcamp Facebook app to sell music right on your Facebook page. *www.bandcamp.com/artists*

Want to sell t-shirts and other band merch? Zazzle offers custom on-demand merchandise with no upfront costs. Sign up for a free account, then upload your artwork and choose the products you want to sell. You can sell your custom merch on your website, through your Facebook page, or on your own Zazzle Store site. Zazzle takes care of manufacturing, inventory and shipping, and you'll earn a royalty rate on every item sold. *www.zazzle.ca*

SOCIAL MEDIA INTEGRATION
(HAVE MORE ONLINE CONVERSATIONS)

Sign up for a free IFTTT account and use it to integrate all your band's social media activities. IFTTT ("IF This Then That") allows you to create simple "recipes" to automate and extend your band's online presence. Choose from over 70 channels, from SoundCloud to Craigslist, and select which "triggers" (e.g., "When my guitarist posts a photo of her gear on Instagram...") should cause what "actions" (e.g. ,"...add the photo to a dedicated album on the band's Facebook page.") *www.ifttt.com*

ORGANIZATIONAL TOOLS
(MANAGE YOUR TIME AND EFFORTS)

A free Google account includes a Gmail address, as well as a Google Calendar. Share your Google Calendar with the rest of your band members and use it to co-ordinate rehearsals, gigs and recording dates. (Google Calendar can be configured to send automatic email and text message reminders too). *www.accounts.google.com*

Sign up for a free online file storage service such as Dropbox and use it as a central place to store your band's promo shots, one-sheets, EPKs and other digital assets. Dropbox is also handy for sharing demo recording, rough mixes, and other large files. *www.dropbox.com*

Finally, how are you going to remember all your passwords for these online services? Sign up for a free LastPass account and use it to safely and conveniently organize all your band's passwords and account information. ● *www.lastpass.com*

If you don't already have your own domain name, you should. Registering "yourbandname.com" will cost you $10-$15 per year. It's a smart and worthwhile investment in securing and strengthening your online presence. You can register a domain name through any reputable domain name registrar.

TIP: If yourbandname.com is unavailable, use http://xona.com/domainhacks/ to search for some clever alternate domain names such as "yourbandna.me".

Once you've registered your domain name, you can choose a shared web hosting provider to host your own website. Shared web hosting is typically the easiest and most cost-effective way to host your own website. A shared web hosting plan from a reputable hosting provider will typically cost between $5-$10 per month.

Visit http://hostcounsel.com/ to search for and compare reputable domain name registrars and web hosting providers.

TIP: If you're not ready to commit to a shared web hosting plan quite yet, choose a domain name registrar that will redirect your domain name to the website of your choice for free. (For example, you may want to redirect yourbandname.com to your band's Facebook page.)

Having your own hosting plan will allow you to install and configure a full-featured web content management system such as WordPress. The self-hosted version of WordPress is completely free, and infinitely more customizable than online blogging platforms such as wordpress.com or blogger.com.

You can also use your hosting plan to set up forward-only email addresses for each of your band members, so that bandmembername@yourbandname.com redirects to each band member's existing email account. You can also set up dedicated email aliases for specific purposes, such as bookings@yourbandname.com or fanmail@yourbandname.com, and redirect emails to the appropriate person in charge. The possibilities are endless. ●

FENIAN FILMS
HAMILTON MUSIC DOCUMENTARY

A local film project that's been in the fire for some time is being actively developed. Ryan Furlong (co-writer, co-producer, and director) and Jeffrey C. Martin (Quorum Communications, co-writer, co-producer) are at the helm of something very exciting with their still-to-be-titled Hamilton music documentary.

"We've been doing research and development for both the story and Furlong's very unique visual approach," said Martin. "We've been writing the director and creative treatments, shooting some preliminary interviews with local musicians for research and screen tests, putting a film budget and book option together, and cultivating strategic relationships with names that include one of the most accomplished executive producers in Hollywood, who has shown an interest in the project for very personal reasons."

The story Furlong and Martin want to tell is as much about a working-class steel town as it is about the musical icons that rose from its streets, stages and recording studios.

"Each of these characters possesses a remarkable gift, but we're not aiming to paint them in technicolor, rather, we want them to appear as they are – real humans who suffer from the same flaws that plague us all," said Furlong. "In some cases these artists have come out alive and with a career while others fell victim to the addictive taste of drugs or booze, the isolation of mental illness, or the unlucky hand that fate often deals. In others, we produced celebrities like Dan Lanois and The Band, not free of their share of burdens, but somehow they came out the other end of the rainbow. Why? That's not to say King Biscuit Boy, Frankie Venom or Ronnie Hawkins didn't have it in them to pick up the hardware (Grammy Awards for example) they just went another way, like the characters in Joyce's 'The Dubliners' perhaps. Hamilton has that effect. Hell, Canada has that effect. I suppose that's why the ones who really "made it" and I mean that in the grand sense, had to escape it first. Jeff and I are more curious about the struggles and missteps, than the obvious successes in the same way I am more interested in the sonic innovations that never became chart toppers but that changed music," said Furlong. "It's far more interesting than a big pat on the back because these stories in our film will be honest, fearless, exciting, and yet accessible to everyone, whether ending at the very top or the very bottom. These individuals took risks."

The documentary's story traces the music scene that evolved in Hamilton from the early '60s to today. The film's logline sums up their vision. "From the streets of a Canadian working class city notorious for its steel mills, infamous gangsters, and blue-collar grit, there evolved some of the most important artists that have come to define popular music as we know it. This documentary unveils their struggles and stories – and gives credit to the colourful musicians who rose to success and others who fell silently behind the scenes." •
www.fenianfilms.com

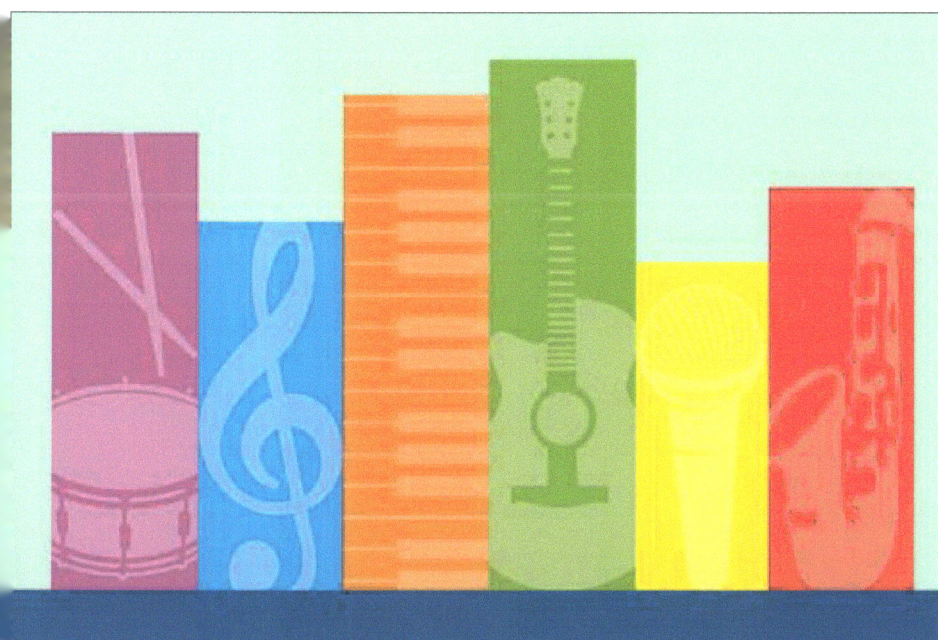

THE CREAM RISES TO THE TOP
2013 HAMILTON MUSIC AWARDS

Lifetime Achievement Award
HARRISON KENNEDY
Lifetime Achievement Award
BORIS BROTT
Music Industry Lifetime Achievement Award
LYMAN POTTS

Recordings of the Year
Adult Contemporary
IAN THOMAS-LITTLE DREAMS
Alt/Country
**JP RIEMENS & THE FABULOUS BARFLIES-
NO FILTER**
Alternative Rock
THE REASON-HOLLOW TREE
Adult Alternative
COWLICK-NIGHT VISION
Blues
HARRISON KENNEDY-SOULSCAPE
Classical
**BUD ROACH-SOSPIRO, ALESSANDRO
GRANDI COMPLETE ARIAS, 1626**
Electronic
JESSY LANZA-PULL MY HAIR BACK

Ethnic/World
YIANNIS KAPOULAS-MYSTIC JOURNEY
Folk/Traditional
**DAWN AND MARRA-
TEASPOONS AND TABLESPOONS**
Instrumental
BRAD CHEESEMAN GROUP-MIXED MESSAGES
Jazz
DIANA PANTON-A CHRISTMAS KISS
Loud/Metal
SHATTERED REMAINS-SHATTERED REMAINS
Punk
TV FREAKS-TWO
Rap/Hip Hop
LEE REED & JOHN P-WRITTEN LARGE
Religious
ROSANNA RIVERSO-THE GIFT OF CHRISTMAS
Rock
MONSTER TRUCK-FURIOSITY
Roots
LEE HARVEY OSMOND-THE FOLK SINNER

Artist of the Year
Female Artist
BUCKSHOT BEBEE
Female Vocalist
DIANA PANTON
Local Group of the Year by People's Choice
JOHN MAMONE
Male Artist
HARRISON KENNEDY
Male Vocalist
HARRISON KENNEDY
New Artist/Group
ALLOTROPE
Producer of the Year
NICK BLAGONA
Record of the Year
MONSTER TRUCK - FURIOSITY
Songwriter of the Year
HARRISON KENNEDY
Studio Engineer of the Year
DARREN MAGIEROWSKI

Music Teacher of the Year (post-secondary)
JAMSHED TUREL, MOHAWK COLLEGE

THRESHOLD RECORDING STUDIO
TEXTURE AND SOUND

Michael Keire is one of Ontario's progressive and dynamic recording engineers and producers. He operates his production studio, Threshold Recording Studio, in Hamilton but also operates freelance across southern Ontario. His studio credits vary in style and genre, ranging from bands such as The Rest, Young Empires, New Hands, Wildlife and Dirty Nil to singer-songwriters like Tom Wilson or Jessy Lanza.

Keire's approach to his craft is a hybrid – technically and philosophically. He's constantly seeking new ways to combine old, more traditional techniques and sounds with modern digital technology. This is manifested in his work. Keire's passion for old saturated records that have amazing dark textures and incredibly three-dimensional sound fields is coupled with the size, detail and immediacy of a modern recording. It also shows in his love for two-inch tape, vintage microphones, spring reverbs and analog delays, but also with his use of the newest digital equipment and computer software. For Keire, it's about searching for great texture and great sounds, no matter where they are.

"After I left my partnership at Vibewrangler, I began to look for new inspirations and connected with pros like mastering guru Brian Lucey (Arctic Monkeys, Black Keys) and producer Joel Hamilton (Pretty Lights, Black Keys, Talib Kweli) in the U.S. Joel is an amazing producer and invited me down to Brooklyn during the Pretty Lights sessions. He's a master of fusing styles and technologies something I've become incredibly passionate about. Reseaching, meeting new people and experimenting is what it's all about."

Working toward developing the creative and progressive merits in music, Keire's approach carries through into his productions, where he's always striving to maintain and build upon the artist's vision and strengths. His engaging, collaborative approach provides an open, easy-going culture in the studio. This has become Threshold's "signature" and can be heard in the records he's made.•
thresholdrecordingstudio.com

PEACE OF MIND ON THE GRAND RIVER
OSHWEKEN'S JUKASA STUDIOS

"THE DIFFERENCE IN COST BETWEEN SOMEONE'S BASEMENT AND WORKING HERE IS NOT AS MUCH AS YOU WOULD THINK"

Darren Magierowski is getting excited as he listens to a track from his latest recording project at Jukasa Studios. Listening to Rees Wynans (Stevie Ray Vaughan, Buddy Guy, Joe Cocker) on the Hammond B3 and piano is blowing him away. "I've been loving working with these guys. They've been in all month, and it's been going great," he says. The rich, exciting sound is testimony of what this world-class studio can produce.

Jukasa Studios is a destination recording facility located in Oshweken five minutes outside of Caledonia, just a few minutes drive down the Sixth Line off of Highway 6. Nearby is the beautiful Grand River, riding stables, some mixed farming, and not much else. It's a peaceful spot located away from the city. The building and property embrace you with their modern, warm and inviting design.

Inside the wood-paneled lobby, platinum records are on display with guitarist/producer Stevie Salas' (Mick Jagger, Sass Jordan, American Idol) name on them. Salas worked at Jukasa when it first opened in 2009. The famous Rolling Stone Magazine cover with the Sheepdogs is nearby. Jukasa has also recorded the likes of Snoop Dogg, Alexisonfire, Protest the Hero, Ill Scarlett, Kobra and the Lotus, Johnny Max Band and Monster Truck.

The control room is laid out in perfect balance, with outboard gear surrounding the legendary 8072 G Series Vintage Analog Console which spent 12 years of its life in studio 3 at Abbey Road Studios. The main tracking room has an attractive acoustic design. A classroom is nearby. The juxtaposition of rural tranquility with cutting edge technology is reminiscent of Le Studio, the environmental studio and retreat in the Laurentians where Rush and April Wine made many records back in the '80s.

Darren Magierowski is now the head engineer at Jukasa Studios. An experienced musician and graduate of the Metalworks Institute, Magierowski will likely prove to be a key component of the studio's ongoing success as it moves into a new phase of growth and outreach. In addition to the recording studio, there is the Jukasa School of Recording Arts, and a soon-to-be opened Dolby Atmos Mix Theatre post-production facility.

HM: You are at the helm of a multi-million operation. What makes it a good fit for you?

DM: It's great. It's a huge opportunity. I went to school for this, worked my ass off, networked. I've played music all my life. I've collected gear, I've toured. I don't feel intimidated by it.

I mesh well with anyone. It's the personnel who work here that make the difference. Without them the studio is just a room of gear. With Mark Capoferri as the head instructor and registrar, it's a great team.

HM: What will it take to maximize the potential of Jukasa Studios?

DM: Awareness is key. I talk to musicians all the time, and they are often surprised to find out that there's a studio out here. We're very close to Hamilton, only 15 minutes away.

I want people to realize that a world-class facility like Jukasa is not much more money than working in your friend's basement. The difference in cost between someone's basement and working here is not as much as you would think.

I'm sensitive to the local market. We will compete not only on cost, but we'll come out on top because of added value. Our situation is different. As a privately owned facility, our goal is to serve not just world class but developing artists too. It's very important for us to be flexible and sensitive to each artist's situation.

HM: What benefits does Jukasa Studios offer and deliver?

DM: I tell everyone, just come out here first. We're 15 minutes from Rymal and Upper James. You're gonna fall in love with it. I like to meet people first. Let's check out the place and the vibe first, then let's talk about what you want to do. Do you want an EP? A single? An entire album? We'll come up with a plan. Sometimes coaching and pre-production work is needed. We're open to that.

We strive to be the place where the artist can be comfortable enough to play well, and take some risks if necessary. Both of these things require a personal commitment from the studio which puts flexibility into the mix. Again, it comes down to the quality of the staff.

We've also had bands come to Jukasa to record videos. Our interior décor and lighting is perfect for certain kinds of shoots.

If an artist needs seclusion, we've got it. If they need convenience, we've got that too. Being close to the Hamilton airport is a great benefit. We've provided limousine service on occasion.

HM: Does it help to have overnight accommodation here?

DM: Big time. Much of our clientele comes >>>

Darren Magierowski is a graduate of the Metalworks Institute. He has toured across Canada and the U.S. with various indie bands spanning more than a decade, working as a backline technician, stage manager, and monitor tech for bands such as Alexisonfire and Kittie.

Darren has worked with world class producers and engineers such as; Julius Butty (Alexisonfire, Protest the Hero), Jim Wirt (Incubus, Fiona Apple), Eric Ratz (Billy Talent, Cancer Bats), Ted Chung (Snoop Lion), Christopher Thorn (Blind Melon), Ben Kaplan (Shakira, Gallows), Matt DeMatteo (Danko Jones, Big Wreck) to name a few. Darren's diverse musical influences and recording experience cover rock, metal, punk, classic rock, folk, country, rockabilly, blues, rap/hip hop, R&B, native traditional, big/swing band, and jazz.

<<< out of the GTA, Brantford, London. We need those accommodations to make it worth their while. A band coming down from Woodbridge that I've worked with a couple of times, wouldn't make the drive if they couldn't stay the night. That's a two hour trek.

Kobra and the Lotus was from Calgary, so having accommodations was vital. Some clients have given positive feedback. They like the vibe, especially in the summer. It's quiet. We sit around the patio, put on the barbecue and have a beer. No lights, sirens, no pressure.

HM: What is Jukasa introducing next?

DM: The Dolby Atmos Mix Theatre will be absolutely fantastic. It's a 3-D high definition surround sound audio/video technology which is the future of movie and video production. We have an agreement with the manufacturers of the Dolby Atmos and AVID that they will ship some new and state of the art equipment to Jukasa first, before anywhere in Canada. We're hoping to open the Mix Theatre early in 2014. This will make Jukasa Media Group the only Dolby Atmos facility in all of Canada.

We're also continuing with our School of Recording Arts. We offer stay-over accommodations during the instructional season, and hands-on training in real-world recording situations.

HM: Anything else you would like to add?

DM: We're excited for the future, and proud to be able to contribute to the Hamilton music scene. Come on out and have a look. Everyone is always welcome! ●

www.jukasamediagroup.com

BIG JOHNNY BLUE
AND THE LITTLE RED BOOK

*Photography **Ivan Sorensen***

There's a small red notebook sitting on Big Johnny Blue's kitchen counter. It's packed full of lyrics and music to original songs, and is the constant companion of its owner. You never know when a new song or lyric idea will hit you. The little red book holds the latest and freshest songs written by Johnny Blue (aka John M. Crawford).

Soon he'll take the book into his cozy home studio to lay down a track. The studio contains several guitars, an electronic keyboard, harmonicas in a variety of keys, and a drum kit.

In the songwriting and music business, life experience enriches and strengthens raw talent. As Charlie Parker once said, "If you don't live it, it won't come out your horn." Big Johnny Blue has the gift of being able to connect with people and make them feel good about themselves, whether he is on stage singing the blues, at home writing a song, or organizing a charitable event.

I caught up with Johnny Blue between sets at the Come By Chance in Hamilton's ground-level East End. He was fronting his trio, Strange Cargo. "It's all about the love of the music, and getting people's emotions to move, and maybe even getting them to move into action," said Johnny Blue.

Big Johnny Blue was involved in the revitalization of the Hamilton Blues Society this year. As president he leads the Blues Society board in promoting blues music in Hamilton at the grassroots level. Monthly jam events at the Knights of Columbus have been steadily growing. The group embraces new technology by live-streaming their jams over the internet. "The technology piece helps us connect with more people. Some aren't just able make it out in person," said Johnny Blue.

It means a growing legion of fans and friends who attend the jams have an opportunity to support community charities. Between September and November, the Hamilton Blues Society supported St. Matthew's House with food bank donations and a toy drive. "It all serves to keep us rooted and connected to the people around us. Kind of what we want our music to do."

At the Come By Chance, Big Johnny Blue was just getting into his second set and there it was: Stormy Monday, the T-Bone Walker classic. After a few seconds it was clear there was no better seat in town than sitting right there, taking in that beautiful song, absorbing its medicine, and feeling all the pain and troubles of life fade away. That's the power of the blues. Thanks Big Johnny Blue for bringing it. And thanks for sharing that little red book of great songs. ●
bigjohnnyblue.bandcamp.com

WORLD MUSIC NOW
MATAPA

"WITH MUSIC FROM AROUND THE WORLD NOW SO EASILY ACCESSIBLE, MATAPA AIMS TO BRING US FACE TO FACE WITH THE MUSIC AND THE CULTURE IN ITS RICHEST, PUREST FORM."

Photography **Cody Lanktree**

Matapa is a local arts promotion organization with a high calling. It aims to broaden our exposure and participation in a wider variety of international musical styles and traditions. Its main strategy is to create an extremely high quality world music series.

According to Matapa board member Dan Medakovic, "There is no other organization in Hamilton that is looking to promote international musical forms to the extent of Matapa."

"Hamilton is a market that is grossly underserved by world music. With something like 55 languages spoken in Hamilton, we're a prime market. Filimone Mabjaia, our director is so committed to all Matapa performances being of topmost quality. That's the thing I like about Matapa. We're creating an opportunity for great musicians to come and perform here."

FAIR COMPENSATION
Medakovic continues, "There are some submandates. We support and respect the musicians as well. All the technical support must be excellent. And the management, communication and compensation must be fair."

The performers are well known in their native countries, so there is a great potential for Matapa shows to draw new audience members on the basis of that cultural connection.

Another portion of the audience for these shows will be local musicians who are open to broadening their horizons and exploring different styles, timbres, time signatures, and techniques. "Throughout the series, we will create opportunities to collaborate with local musicians to back up visiting headliners, and vice-versa. Last year Trinity Mpho's backing band had Joel Banks as the bass player. The keyboard player was Bruce Tournay. They hadn't played that kind of music before. And recently, we featured local songstress Terra Lightfoot, collaborating with several musicians including Zal Sissokho (African kora/harp master) and Irshad Kahn (sitar)."

The Matapa opportunities for collaboration will bring the musicians themselves together, and have an enduring, enriching effect on the artist.

Medakovic hopes to help create some recordings of these collaborative, international efforts. "One idea is to take the singer-songwriter crowd that I'm connected with and have them work with international musicians. They could strip down the music and rebuild it in a collaborative effort. Then there are potential touring opportunities that could follow."

CULTURAL EXCHANGES
Matapa also has a long-term goal of setting up musician exchanges. For example, a Hamilton artist would be identified and have the exciting opportunity to have expenses paid for a musical exchange trip to Botswana, Mozambique or southern Africa.

Filimone, who is from Mozambique, has extensive experience in that region of Africa as a concert promoter and has great connections with world-class acts. "Now that we have our concert series in place, the most immediate goal is to increase local audience sizes and find financial sponsors. The task of getting the word around and putting people into seats is the priority now. People don't know what they're missing."

INTERNATIONAL HAMILTON WORLD MUSIC FESTIVAL
Matapa is planning a mid-summer festival. "Our festival next July will be a weekend of world music, food, and craft at the Waterfront Park," says Filimone. "We're calling it something like the Hamilton World Music Festival." With music from around the world now so easily accessible, it is too easy to ignore the finer details of what the cultural origins may be. Matapa aims to bring us face to face with the music and the culture in its richest, purest form. ●

For a list of upcoming shows and tickets, or more information in general, please visit Matapa.ca.

Music Ontario

In a band?
Work in music?
MusicOntario is here to help

MusicOntario is a membership-based non-profit organization with a mission to provide education, professional development, information & support to the music industry in Ontario.

We deliver a number of events and services throughout the year, including:

- Workshops
- Networking Events
- Consultations
- Newsletter
- Members Discount Program
- Advocacy and more!

For more, visit **www.music-ontario.ca** | @MusicOntario | facebook.com/MusicOntario

MusicOntario is a division of the Canadian Independent Music Association CIMA

matapa
music & arts organization

DECEMBER 7TH
LEMON BUCKET ORCHESTRA

JANUARY 11TH
SULTANS OF STRING

MARCH 8TH
ELEANOR DUBINSKY
THE VOICE OF SAVANAH,
FEIHONG
LIL ACEVEDO
*(COLABORATION FOR
INTERNATIONAL WOMENS' DAY)*

APRIL 5TH
CARMEN SOUZA
(DIRECT FROM CAPE VERDE)
& WAZIMBO
(DIRECT FROM MOZAMBIQUE)

2nd annual Roots en Route FESTIVAL

FEBRUARY 2ND TO 8TH, 2014

FEBRUARY 2ND
OPEN NIGHT WITH
FATOUMATA DIAWARA (MALI)
& MICHAEL ST. GEROGE (JAMAICA/HAMILTON)

TICKETS AVAILABLE NOW!
TICKETMASTER AND MATAPA.CA

MORE INFORMATION AND FULL PROGRAM:
INFO@MATAPA.CA OR VISIT WWW.MATAPA.CA

CHCH
Your Superstation

THE HAMILTON SPECTATOR
thespec.com

FUN TIMES AT
THE ZOO-PERCRAWL
THE JOY OF LEARNING
A MUSICAL INSTRUMENT
By Chris Cowsill & John Best

"WE SOON REALIZED THAT WE HAD TO DO SOMETHING MORE THAN JUST SHOW THE CHILDREN MUSICAL INSTRUMENTS ONCE A YEAR AND THEN LEAVE."

If you were at Hamilton's Supercrawl this past September and heard what sounded like an out-of-control orchestra tuning up, odds are you were passing by the "Instrument Petting Zoo." The sounds you heard were budding young musicians sampling a range of orchestral instruments. The booth was there to get the word out about "An Instrument For Every Child" (AIFEC), a local charitable organization that is all about giving children the opportunity to experience the joy of learning a musical instrument.

The AIFEC program starts with children in grade one being introduced to a variety of instruments through hands-on demonstrations by volunteers from Hamilton's music community. Then, in grade two, the kids receive lessons on the instrument of their choice with qualified instructors. And soon the kids can play some basic melodies. Small ensembles start in grade three but the program ends at grade four. At this time, we hope a program can be established with the Hamilton Philharmonic Orchestra to mentor promising young musicians. All of this is provided free of charge by the program and instruments are made available for the students to take home to practice on.

"An Instrument For Every Child is not just another music project," says program founder Astrid Hepner. "It is a social project at heart, and we are excited that AIFEC is becoming a reality in Hamilton. AIFEC doesn't set out to produce world-class musicians. Rather, it hopes to create community spirit by giving children the opportunity to develop teamwork and interpersonal relationship skills through music."

The idea came to Hepner after the Jazz in the Hubs outreach program where the Mohawk College Jazz Band played at dozens of local schools, sponsored by the Hamilton Music Collective. Children were excited by the hands-on component of the program where they got to try the instruments. "We soon realized that we had to do something more than just show the children musical instruments once a year and then leave," said Hepner. She turned to her native Germany, where a program was established to provide instruments and music lessons to elementary schools. "We used that program as a template," she said.

Through a fortunate set of circumstances, Hepner was put in touch with Paul Lloyd, who had remembered the value he obtained as an inner city kid by being able to play in a band. It was Paul's donation of $150,000 that launched the AIFEC program. Since then, other sponsors have come aboard, including ArcelorMittal, the Hamilton Community Foundation, the Trillium Fund and the Turkstra Family Foundation. Currently the program is operating in six schools: Cathy Wever, Hess Street, Holy Name of Jesus, Dr. Davey, Memorial and Prince of Wales. The goal is to be in 10 schools by 2015.

Astrid Hepner's career has taken some fascinating turns. Born and educated in Germany, she studied Musicology at the University of Cologne and earned her degree in Performing Arts from the Folkwang School in Essen. An accomplished saxophonist, she moved to New York City in 1995 with her husband Darcy Hepner, a Hamilton native. She worked in the music business as a performer and bandleader, and in marketing for EMI Records and The Blue Note Group. Both Hepners are currently instructors within Mohawk College's music program.

If the Instrument Petting Zoo comes to a location near you, stop in and introduce yourself. Think of the value of AIFEC. The anticipation of children joyfully playing a musical instrument makes it worth spending time amongst the bleating of the saxophone, the mooing of the trombone, the growling of the bass and the beating of the drums. •

Support the **Gift of Music** in Hamilton Schools

Help Hamilton's inner-city kids build self-esteem and empower them to reach their full potential by learning to play a musical instrument.

Tom Wilson (Three-time Juno Winner)

"*An Instrument For Every Child* creates opportunities and helps kids develop their own creativity. I believe that inspiring children to become artists is only going to make a better community and as a result a better world."

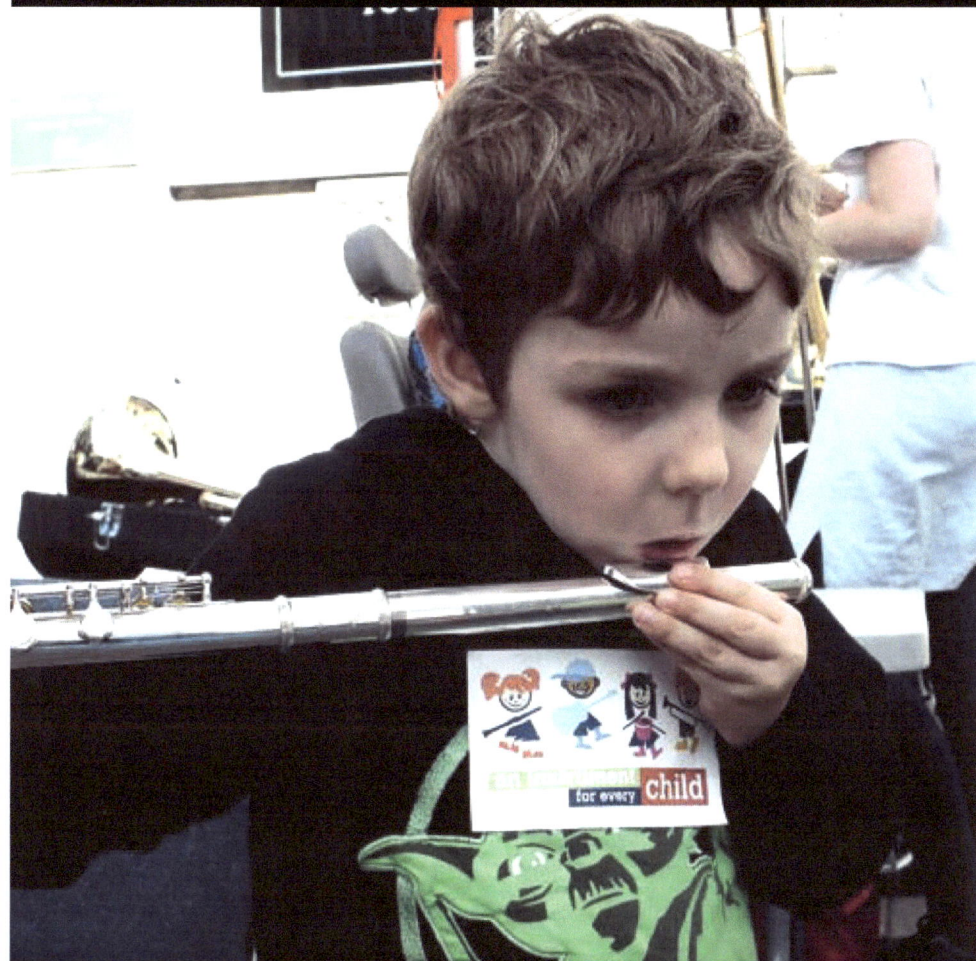

Photography by Cathie Coward

an instrument for every child

HAMILTON MUSIC COLLECTIVE

Programming Partner
HAMILTON PHILHARMONIC ORCHESTRA

Media Partners
OKD MARKETING

THE HAMILTON SPECTATOR
thespec.com

AN INTERVIEW WITH
ZIMFIRA POLOZ
ARTISTIC DIRECTOR OF
THE HAMILTON CHILDREN'S CHOIR
By David Fawcett

"I KNOW IF I WERE BACK HOME (IN KAZAKHSTAN) WE WOULD WORK THROUGH THE WHOLE SUMMER INTENSIVELY. IN CANADA, IT IS TRICKY TO ASK FOR SUCH COMMITMENT."

*Photography **Cormac Figgis***

I spoke with Zimfira Poloz, the Artistic Director of the Hamilton Children's Choir (HCC), a cluster of four graduated choirs and a Kindersing program for three- to six-year olds. Poloz was educated in Kazakhstan where she became the principal and conductor of the country's first choir school. She has a distinguished international reputation as clinician and adjudicator and has worked in those capacities around the world.

In the course of our conversation, Poloz noted that the HCC is better known internationally than here at home in Hamilton. It became clear that her primary commitment is to music education. "I hope that someone will recognize the value of the choirs and sponsor them because I think every child, regardless of their means, should be able to join if they want," said Poloz. She voices her hope that more teachers in the school systems will encourage their students to join the HCC, in addition to choirs in their home schools. Poloz also put out the call for adult volunteers to help share the load.

I asked her about the Chamber Choir's recent trip to Guangzhou, China where they won the 5000 1st Xinghai Prize in the International Choir Championships.

GHM: How were you invited? How did Interkultur, the German organization that runs these international events, learn about the HCC?

ZP: We have sung at big international events and people know about the Hamilton Children's Choir. In recent years, we've performed at the Let the Future Sing festival in Sweden and won the Children Choir Category of the Let the People Sing Euroradio Competition. We were invited as a guest choir to do some special concerts and to sing at the opening ceremony. At the last minute, I decided to ask if it was possible to compete. It was a great experience.

GHM: How long was the trip to China? Where did you stay? What did you eat? Teenaged girls might not be very adventurous.

ZP: It was such a long journey. I think it was 16 hours altogether. We had a direct flight from Toronto to Hong Kong and then we changed to fly to Guangzhou. We stayed in a hotel. Because we were invited, we were accommodated by Interkultur who staged the event with the Chinese choral organization.

The first day we had a very shocking food experience. The people were trying to be so nice and the food was so different from what are kids were used to. They were very polite and tried everything. There was a lot of rice. By the second day they started to change the menu to things we were more used to. We had a European style breakfast at the hotel, but the other meals were served at a very big centre where all the choirs came to eat. It gave the children a chance to see each other and talk to each other. That was a great, fun experience.

GHM: Where were the other choirs from?

ZP: There were 7,000 singers. Choirs from all over the world. They came from Russia, Latvia, Russia, Sweden, Colombia, Mexico, The Philippines. There was a lot of diversity. Choirs of all sorts: male choirs, mixed choirs, women's choirs, and children's choirs.

GHM: How was the trip funded?

ZP: We took about 36 choristers and five adults. There was very little cost in China so it was mostly the airfare, which also was subsidized by the Chinese. It worked out to about $2000 per child, paid by their families.

GHM: Where did you sing?

ZP: We sang at the opening ceremony at the Guangzhou Opera House. It was huge and it was a sold out concert. We had just arrived and the kids were so tired they wanted to lie down and sleep on the floor. This was a unique event that it sold out so quickly they made the dress rehearsal a performance. Otherwise, people from the other choirs, who had come so far, wouldn't get to hear it.

GHM: Did you hear other choirs there? How good were they?

ZP: We were so busy with our rehearsals and performance that we heard very little. The opening ceremony we couldn't see because we were in it. The closing ceremony we were able to see. We also did concerts with other choirs.

I wish we could have 12 hours of rehearsal (like they do). It's quite intense to work in such a situation. I know, I was the founder of such a choir school. I know if I were back home (in Kazakhstan) we would work through the whole summer intensively. In Canada it is tricky to ask for such commitment. As it is, I teach everything: theory, sight singing, vocal production, and life skills in four hours a week.

GHM: So what's next for the HCC?

ZP: We have a number of high top standard international opportunities and are considering a high level tour. Unfortunately, even if we are accepted, we may not be able to afford to go.

The big project next year is a concert with the Hamilton Philharmonic Orchestra. It is always a good opportunity for the children to sing with a professional orchestra.

There'll be a very engaging production in the spring with the chamber choir for which we are seeking an interesting performance venue. It will be a theatrical production to push boundaries a little bit and develop a story connecting the songs throughout the concert. ●
hamiltonchildrenschoir.org

ORCHESTRAL MANEOUVRES
A BRIEF HISTORY OF THE DUNDAS VALLEY ORCHESTRA
By Peter Hill

"THE FIRST ORCHESTRA CONSISTED OF A WIDE RANGE OF PEOPLE, FROM MUSIC TEACHERS TO STEELWORKERS, FROM DOCTORS TO THE UNEMPLOYED."

Arthur Vogt founded the Dundas Valley Orchestra (DVO) in the fall of 1978 by. Vogt was born and raised in Hamilton and after graduating from McMaster University, enjoyed a career of teaching music in several cities across Ontario. He returned to Dundas after retiring in 1975. Though active as a church organist and choir director, Vogt decided he needed more to keep him busy so he developed a vision for a community orchestra that would be a 'players' orchestra."

Vogt created a three-part mission for the new orchestra:

1. To preserve the art of orchestral music playing by allowing amateur musicians to experience the joy of performing in an orchestra and at the same time, maintain and improve their talents.
2. To have the orchestra be of service to the community by entertaining at local retirement homes.
3. To give young and promising music students a chance (in many cases their first opportunity) to solo with an orchestra.

The first orchestra consisted of a wide range of people, from music teachers to steelworkers, from doctors to the unemployed, and spanned ages from high school students to retired people from the Greater Hamilton area.

The repertoire was to be classical works with some modern orchestral works, including show tunes. The first concert was held in the spring of 1979 and, according to Art, was quite terrible. The first concerts were affectionately called the LAUFAR Concerts, which were largely attended by "Loving And Understanding Friends And Relatives."

The DVO has performed two free concerts annually ever since. Free concerts are also performed at four retirement and nursing homes annually, and numerous concertos have been performed featuring promising young musicians.

When Art Vogt retired as conductor, we discovered the orchestra was not only a desirable venue for amateur musicians but also for aspiring conductors. SHOULD BE A REFERENCE HERE TO ADJACENT SIDEBAR

The DVO has had various practice venues over the years, the music rooms of Highland and Parkside secondary schools, the "Old" Baptist Church in Dundas and its current home, the Centre for String Playing on Main Street West. Practices are held on Tuesday nights from 7:30 to 9:30 p.m. The orchestra performs its two annual concerts usually in Dundas churches but also in other venues in the Hamilton area.

In 2003, the DVO celebrated its 25th Anniversary and a celebration concert featured a guest appearance of Arthur Vogt. It is a charitable organization and receives a modest City of Hamilton Community Partnership Grant. The remainder of its budget comes from member donations and generous donations from concert patrons and program advertisers.

The Dundas Valley Orchestra's mission set out by Art Vogt 35 years ago remains strong and valid today. DVO continues to work with young musicians, and in 2012, instituted a Student Composer Competition and performed the winning composition at its Spring Concert in 2013. The competition is an annual one and for 2013 the Hamilton AM Rotary Club sponsored a $250 cash prize for the winner.

The orchestra also has assisted the Mohawk College Music Department for the last two years in the role of back-up orchestra for several of the school's amazing soloists, both voice and instrument at their year-end performance.

The DVO welcomes any musician, new or established, who may want to join the orchestra, and encourages all young musicians to learn more about it's Student Composer Competition.●
Visit DVO's website for further details.
www.dundasvalleyorchestra.ca

Listed below is the chronology of Dundas Valley Orchestra conductors and some of their achievements.

1978 - 1990

Arthur Vogt, high school music teacher, founder of the Dundas Valley Orchestra, also founded two local choirs, the Albertones and Silver Bells.

1990 - 1992

Peter Hughes was a high school music teacher, and conductor of numerous bands and orchestras in the Hamilton area. Peter died of a heart attack a few days after DVO's spring concert in 1992. The orchestra played at his funeral.

1992 - 1994

Michael Hall, formerly resident conductor of the Winnipeg Symphony Orchestra and the Winnipeg Youth Orchestra, became conductor of the South West Florida Symphony (Tampa).

1994 - 1996

Rosemary Thomson became the music director of the Okanagan Symphony Orchestra, chorus master of the Calgary Philharmonic and Assistant Conductor for the Canadian Opera Company.

1996 - 1997

Stéphan Potvin was former director of the Hamilton Male Orpheus Choir.

1997 - 2011

Dr. Glenn Mallory was former conductor of the Hamilton Youth Philharmonic Orchestra (42 years) and retired director of music with the Hamilton Board of Education.

2011 - PRESENT

Laura Thomas is also active as the associate conductor of the Niagara Symphony Orchestra, music director of the Niagara Youth Orchestra, and artistic director of the Hamilton/Niagara area WomEnchant Chorus.

DUNDAS VALLEY ORCHESTRA
FOUNDED IN 1978

DO YOU PLAY AN INSTRUMENT?
NEED A GROUP TO PLAY WITH?
WE INVITE COMMITTED AMATEURS TO JOIN US

OUR NEXT FREE CONCERT IS ON SUN JANUARY 19TH 2014
AT ST PAUL'S UNITED CHURCH DUNDAS AT 3PM

LEARN MORE AT WWW.DUNDASVALLEYORCHESTRA.CA

Dundas Valley Orchestra

MUSICIAN/BAND FOR HIRE

Portable project recording studio. Percussionist and children's edutainer for hire.
daverobgould@gmail.com
www.reverbnation.com/davegould.

Jason Hales - performer, trained singer, entertainer, 20 yrs experience available for corporate events, parties, live entertainment, lessons, weddings, classical, light rock, musical theatre, friendly personality.
www.jasonhales.ca jasonhales@gmail.com
416-565-9490

Pip offers a musically sophisticated set of original artpop with a jazz inflection. He will play live for your event and bring his p.a. if necessary. Stream his tunes at MetroPhilMusic.bandcamp.com
contact him at MetroPhilMusic@gmail.com

Andre Bisson & The J-Tones - 5-Piece Rhythm & Blues, Funk, Rock, Swing and Soul Band Available for all events.
www.andrebisson.ca 905-741-1837

Brenda Brown - professional singer. Beautiful Music For Your Special Occasion. Receptions, ceremonies, banquets, cocktails. Jazz standards, American songbook, pop.
www.brendabrownmusic.com

David Lum - Singer/songwriter/guitar/bass/mandolin available for live performances and studio work.
289-441-6512 davidgwlum@hotmail.com
www.davidlum.com

Professional drummer (retired) and teacher with more than 40 years experience. Now accepting a limited number of students. Oakville
905-844-2379 / rwdbest@gmail.com

Doug Feaver, singer/guitar/harmonica solo performer for hire, also plays drums and bass, quick study, rock, country, folk, blues. Live/studio. Lessons also available.
dougfeavermusic@gmail.com

"Fairlane" Seniors Entertainment: Popular top hits from radio, TV and variety shows, from 1950 to 1962. Unique duo with two vocals, two guitars. Our show at your location. Advance bookings:
kenhammond.music@gmail.com 905-634-1522

Try SMOOTH BLEND to add the thrill of live Cocktail Jazz to your next party or reception. Contact Ralph
905-512-6713 ralph.lefevre@shaw.ca

Tony G - Vocalist and guitarist performing great songs of the '60s and '70s, classics for seniors and music for weddings and sacred services.
tonygmusician@gmail.com.

The Diamond Drapes – '50s rock 'n' roll (such as Carl Perkins, Gene Vincent, Chuck Berry, Elvis, etc.) Find us on Facebook and Youtube.
plyth53@gmail.com

COWLICK Check out http://www.cowlick.ca/MUSIC.html for our album "Wires" FREE and more. Our new EP, "Night Vision" is out now and available at Dr. Disc Hamilton and on iTunes.

Free music downloads from one of Hamilton's finest singer/songwriters, Dan Medakovic.
www.reverbnation.com/danmedakovic

The Gunter Ott Band plays laid back blues and roots rock that blends Delta, Chicago and hardscrabble Hamilton grit. Bookings: (905) 544-9194 or gunter.ott@sympatico.ca

MUSICAL ORGANIZATIONS

Symphony on the Bay presents Schumann and our Young Musicians: Sunday, November 3rd, 3 :00 p.m. at the Burlington Performing Arts Centre.
905-681-6000

EQUIPMENT FOR SALE

JBL Eon 15 powered PA for sale with JBL Eon powered 10 for monitors, stands for all; Yamaha 6 ch. mixer, rack with 30 band eq., echo; 2 acoustic violins (1 has pickup); 1 Yamaha solid body elec. "silent violin" with cases for all; a 1964 Strat; a 1965 Fender P bass; SWR 15 bass amp; Fender bass amp and a set of electric drums. For info/prices call Reg at 905-538-8576.

MUSICAL SERVICES

Crash Landing Music, 1189 Cannon St. East @ Ottawa St. Hamilton. 905 548 0039

Steve's Violin Repair has been providing a complete repair service and parts for violins, violas, cellos and basses since 1995. Call 905-547-7116 or 905-518-0433.

Toneland is a studio for music lessons, rehearsals and recording. Our hope is to help everyone achieve their musical goals. Come have some fun.
tonelandstudio.com

Ivan Sorensen Photography. Bands, musicians, portraiture, promo and live event photography.
www.ivansorensenphotography.com

Euphonious Radio. A web radio station with a "music mix like no other," featuring Indie, Classic Rock, Jazz, Blues and more. Broadcasting from Brantford.
www.euphonious.ca

Infinite Music Guitar Lessons. Learn the music you want to play from a professional musician with over 20 years of teaching and performing experience. New students at all levels from beginner to pros who want to push their guitar playing to the level.
Call today. 905-318-6642

LIVE MUSIC VENUES

Brantford Music Centre is an authorized Fender, Gretsch, Guild, Peavey, Yahama and Jackson dealer with a full drum department. In-house tube amp and guitar repair.
422 Colborne St. East in Brantford.
www.musicentre.com

The Pearl Company Arts Centre: The finest in live Music Concerts, Art & Theatre in your backyard! ARTBus. Superfine acoustics. Affordable pricing!
www.thepearlcompany.ca

Acoustic Blend Cafe - Is a volunteer run concert series that promotes local performers from the Greater Hamilton Area. Each concert is followed by Open Mic.
www.facebook.com/AcousticBlendCafe
acousticblendcafe@gmail.com 905-522-1323

MUSIC SCHOOLS

Hamilton Conservatory of the Arts, 126 James Street South, Hamilton, ON. Music lessons for all ages. Continuing an artistic tradition in Hamilton since 1905.
Tel. 905 528-4020 info@hcarts.ca

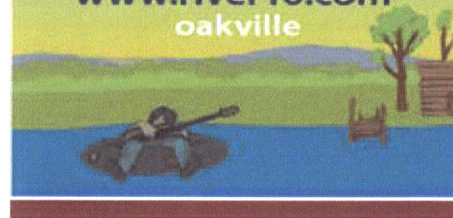